The Novel Too

The Novel Today

A Critical Guide to the British Novel 1970–1989

Allan Massie

Longman (London and New York)

In association with
The British Council

LONGMAN GROUP UK LIMITED,
Longman House, Burnt Mill, Harlow,
Essex CM20 2JE, England
and Associated Companies throughout the world.

*Published in the United States of America
by Longman Inc., New York*

First published 1990

British Library Cataloguing in Publication Data
Massie, Allan, *1938 –*
  The novel today: a critical guide to the British novel, 1970–1989.
  1. Fiction in English, 1945–   . Critical studies
  I. Title
  823.91409

ISBN 0-582-00407-1

Library of Congress Cataloging-in-Publication Data
Massie, Allan, 1938–
  The novel today: a critical guide to the British novel, 1970–1989
  Allan Massie.
    p.   cm.
  Includes bibliographical references.
  ISBN 0-582-00407-1
  1. English fiction — 20th century — History and criticism.
I. Title.
PR881.M387   1990   89–13892
823'.91409 — dc20   CIP

Set in 10/12 Linotron 202 Bembo

Produced by Longman Group (FE) Limited
Printed in Hong Kong

Contents

List of Illustrations

The Publishers are grateful to the Author's Agents for
permission to reproduce an extract from *The Honorary Consul*
by Graham Greene (pubd. The Bodley Head Ltd. 1973).
Copyright © Graham Greene 1973.

1

The novel today

The title of this essay begs definition and poses questions. There is no such thing as 'the novel today'; there are only novels. Several hundred works of fiction of some literary merit are published every year. They are tangible objects which may be read. 'The novel', on the other hand, cannot be read; it is an idea, an abstraction. As such, it is not even the Platonic idea of which individual novels are shadowy representations. Indeed the reverse is more nearly true. It is 'the novel' which represents a concept formed as a result of reading a great many quite distinct novels. All talk of 'the novel' is inevitably generalization, made more impressive, but perhaps less significant, the further it is removed from consideration of particular works of fiction.

Whether a book is a novel may itself be a matter of dispute. There is no satisfactory definition of a novel. Books have been published as novels in one country and as non-fiction in another. I have concluded it is sensible to consider a book as a novel if its publisher has offered it as such.

This survey excludes fiction written in foreign languages and novels first published in the United States. What should properly come within its scope is a difficult question. The Booker-McConnell Prize, which was established in 1969 and which has contributed to a revival of public interest in fiction, is open to novels written by citizens of the United Kingdom, the Commonwealth, and the Republics of South Africa, Ireland and Pakistan, if written in English and first published in the United Kingdom. Of the eighty different novelists short-listed for the prize since its inception, at least a quarter are not British citizens. The prize is indeed imperial in conception; eligibility is conferred by citizenship of any country which was within the British Empire a hundred years ago. On the whole I have found it convenient to adhere to this liberal, if illogical, criterion.

For one thing is clear: it is no longer possible to impose narrow national categories on the novel. Thirty years ago it was still possible to write of 'the English novel'; such a title would no longer make sense.

Twenty years is not necessarily a long time in terms of a novelist's career. Graham Greene, for instance, published his first novel in 1929 and his twenty-fifth in 1988. Anthony Powell's first novel, *Afternoon Men*, appeared in 1931; *The Fisher King* in 1986.

Clearly Greene and Powell are exceptional examples of longevity and the survival of talent. Death, illness, insanity, liquor, financial failure, disappointment, the malediction of critics, loss of ability, or the decay of ambition, truncate many careers. Nevertheless, in spite of all, a writing life of thirty or forty years is common. Any survey of two decades must at least take note of many writers whose reputation was established long before the commencement of the period under review.

However sceptical one may be of the value of speaking about 'the novel', it is difficult to write about fiction without giving some sort of assent to that abstraction. Twenty years ago it was fashionable to speculate about 'the death of the novel'. It would, we were told, become an art-form that pleased only a minority; like poetry. All forms of art of course appeal only to a minority of people, but it seemed plausible then to maintain that the novel had surrendered its primacy as a means of conveying imaginative experience. In 1975, in his introduction to *Beyond the Words: Eleven Writers in Search of a New Fiction*, Giles Gordon wrote that 'fiction is no longer a popular art'. Few would now agree. The recovery may have owed something to the introduction of prizes and the consequent heightening of public awareness. It has owed more to novelists themselves, and to their ability to address themselves to interesting themes in a sufficiently interesting manner.

In 1977 Malcolm Bradbury edited a collection of essays on *The Novel Today*. He found that 'many novelists today have become uneasy with the code of old fictional expectations, with the established history of the novel, and have sought to re-experience and re-make the form by enquiring into its essentials'. The codes of which he wrote had come from two sources. There was realism, emphasizing plot and character, and drawing its strength from a 'real' world beyond the novel; and there was the 'modernist aesthetics of the earlier part of the

2

century, in which "pattern", "form", and "myth" assumed a paramount importance'. Both these modes had, he thought, ceased to satisfy writers, and he identified two responses to this dissatisfaction.

The first was a withdrawal from the established mode 'towards the lexical surface of the text' which 'becomes the sufficient event'. The second 'related phenomenon' was 'a fascination with the fictional process as a parody of form – it becomes the games-like construct with which permutations can be played'.

This was a widely held academic view of the state of the novel. However intelligent the analysis, its expression in this manner was likely to confirm the suspicion of the reader that the novel had been cornered by literary theorists. Certainly novels susceptible of such analysis were not likely to appeal to many readers.

Nevertheless the claim that experiment of one sort or another was the way of the future appeared persuasive. Giles Gordon then seemed content to accept that 'novel writing and reading' should become 'a more private elitist activity than hitherto'; Bradbury judged that 'the experimental potential of the novel has been strongly emphasized by contemporary English novelists, and has markedly intensified in the later 1960s and early 1970s'. How a 'potential' can 'intensify' puzzles me, but I am ready to accept that this is how it seemed then.

Both were writing in reaction to a categorization of the post-war English novel as offering, in Gordon's words, 'unambitious but competent slice-of-life mediocrity'. Though both agreed that this was too facile a judgement, Bradbury yet quoted with approval Bernard Bergonzi's opinion that 'the English novel is no longer novel', offering only 'predictable pleasures'.

Since then the confidence that the novel required to be revitalized by self-conscious experiment has waned. B. S. Johnson, the most interesting of the English experimentalists, whose work combined verbal inventiveness with structural, even typographical, innovation, killed himself in 1973, an act which in retrospect takes on a sad symbolic importance. Subsequent innovators have been tamer. A few such as Salman Rushdie have borrowed from the techniques of Latin American 'Magic Realists' with a success that already seems flashy rather than substantial. D. M. Thomas in *The White Hotel* (1988) mixed poetry, psychoanalysis in the form of case-studies and exchanges between doctor and patient, reportage, and borrowings from other writers, concocting a brew which intoxicated some critics and intrigued many readers; his subsequent novels, written in the same manner, have seemed simultaneously thin and woolly, the lack of any true seriousness being apparent. At best they offer a portrait of the author rather than of the world.

Meanwhile more whole-hearted experimentalists like Christine Brooke-Rose and Giles Gordon himself seem to have abandoned the novel: her last book was *Thru* (1975) and his *Ambrose's Vision* (1981). Others like Emma Tennant have moved back into the mainstream. So has Anthony Burgess, who could in 1970 have been considered experimental on the strength of *The Clockwork Orange* (1962); his best novels *Earthly Powers* (1980) and *Any Old Iron* (1989) are the sort of 'baggy monster' which Henry James deplored as quintessentially English. Burgess has written illuminatingly about James Joyce; but *Earthly Powers* in particular recalls writers like Bennett, Wells, Galsworthy and Maugham, rather than Joyce.

An even more remarkable case is that of William Golding. His critical reputation has been high since his first novel *Lord of the Flies* appeared in 1954. With the exception of that book, which quickly, partly on account of its subject-matter, became a standard school-text, his novels were long regarded as 'difficult'; they attracted academics because they offered problems of exegesis. Throughout most of the 1970s he published nothing. Then came *Darkness Visible* (1979), a Miltonic novel (as the title suggests), being an exploration of the nature of good and evil. In it he employed time-shifts, indirect narration and multiple points of view. It was technically brilliant: shafts of dazzling light were emitted from obscure cloud. But, after this, Golding wrote a trilogy, a historical pastiche, about a voyage from England to Australia, the first volume of which, *Rites of Passage,* won the Booker Prize in 1980. Between the first and second volumes appeared *The Paper Men* (1984), a comedy about the pursuit of a celebrated author by an obtuse but determined biographer. All these books were more immediately accessible than any of his earlier work.

The cases of Golding and Burgess are significant and exemplary. Novelists have, at least for the moment, declined to allow the novel to be steered into the backwater of a minority art-form. They have guided it back into the mainstream. Bradbury himself, though the academic proponent of experiment, is a conventional novelist. *The History Man* (1975) and *Rates of Exchange* (1982), his two best novels, are both firmly in an English comic tradition, the first being a fine and acute example of the provincial university novel, deriving from *Lucky Jim,* the second – despite fashionable references to what he calls 'sado-monetarism' – belonging essentially to a familiar vein: the hero is an English innocent abroad who finds foreigners comic, perplexing and frightening.

A similar change of temper can be remarked in the novels of Muriel Spark. She began as a sharp, funny and disconcerting observer of bourgeois life, with novels like *Memento Mori* (1959) and *The Bachelors* (1960), which attracted the admiring attention of Evelyn Waugh. Then in the late 1960s and early 1970s, she published a succession of novellas in which description was reduced to the minimum necessary for her immediate atmospheric purpose, and which achieved the dislocating clarity of dream. In all these books natural order is disturbed, most evidently in *The Hothouse by the East River* (1973), in which nothing is as it seems to be: the principal characters, living in the New York of the early 1970s where 'sick is interesting, sick is real', were, we learn, killed by a flying bomb in London in 1944, and it is their alternative unlived lives of which we read. In *Not to Disturb* (1971) everything which is going to happen in the novel has already happened in the minds of the characters: the servants in a château in Switzerland know that their master and mistress, and the secretary who has been lover to both, will die by murder and suicide, before the deaths have taken place, and have accordingly sold their stories to the world's press and arranged for the arrival of the television cameras. These novels are probably the finest examples of Magic Realism in English. (The term Magic Realism is discussed in more detail on pages 54–5).

Yet in the five novels she has published since 1976 Muriel Spark has abandoned this sort of experiment with time and structure. Her fiction, though still original and unsettling, has nevertheless again positioned itself in the 'real' world of sense and society. She has eschewed the oddity with which she flirted. Her latest novels affirm the truth of what the French critic Nathalie Sarraute (herself the author of some of the most interesting examples of the *nouveau roman*) wrote in *L'Ère du Soupçon:* 'the traditional novel retains an eternal youthfulness; its generous and flexible form can still, without resorting to any major change, adapt itself to all the new stories, all the new characters and all the new conflicts which develop within successive societies. And it is in the novelty of characters and conflicts that the principal interest and the only worthwhile renewal of the novel can be found.'

Why has this happened? Undoubtedly the resurgence of the traditional novel and the weakening of interest in formal experiment are connected with changes in publishing which have taken place in the last twenty years. The writing of novels can never be divorced from the means by which they are published and the readership to which they are directed. It might even be said that nothing has been more important in determining the sort of novels that are written than the recovery by publishers of the belief that they can sell novels in sufficient quantities to be profitable. This is itself partly the result of changes which have taken place within the publishing business itself; changes popularly expressed in the opinion that it has become more a business and less a way of life. Publishers seem to believe more than ever that the success of a book depends on the way it is marketed, and they have therefore demanded a product which they can direct to a wider market. The new respectability of money has benefited authors too. Agents, who have become more important in the last twenty years, have been able to extract from publishers unprecedentedly high advances. (Anthony Burgess has remarked that authors used to live on their royalties, but now live on advances.) Having paid these, publishers are compelled to make more strenuous efforts to sell books. Those who fail to do lose both money and authors.

One might observe, since it is undoubtedly relevant to the condition of the novel today, that there is no evidence for the fear, frequently expressed, that this new commercialism makes it more difficult for new authors to be published. Common sense, as well as observation of other businesses, should convince anyone that no business-like publisher can continue to thrive if he does not find new authors as his old ones die, grow stale, or lose their popular appeal in a changing market. To employ the language of other trades, continuing success depends on the ability to develop and promote new lines and new products. It seems likely that an informal system will evolve whereby first and probably second novels will be brought out by small independent houses which will then lose the more successful of their authors to the conglomerates able to offer bigger advances. This will be unfortunate for the original publishers, but there is no persuasive reason to think it more generally harmful either to authors or to literature.

This development has encouraged the move back to the mainstream. In general a novel which is going to sell to a mass market must be accessible. (The quality common to almost all commercial bestsellers is ease of reading.) Brian Moore and William Boyd are two novelists who have recognized the importance of accessibility. Both are serious writers prepared to explore difficult and important subjects, but they realize that people read novels for pleasure, not out of duty. They are lucid and engaging; they tell a good story and create convincing characters. It is partly a question of good manners, but it is also a consequence of a reviving faith in the popularity of novels. The writer who is not confined to writing for a small number of like-minded people will aim for lucidity.

It is possible to push this argument too far. There are two reasons. First, the most commercially minded publisher may yet realize that a market exists for certain types of experiment: Russell Hoban, Salman Rushdie, D. M. Thomas and Martin Amis have all had great success with books that might be called experimental, though one might add that Amis's last novel *Money* (1984) was much more immediately accessible and obviously entertaining than its predecessor *Other People* (1981). Yet the right sort of novelty – an admittedly indeterminate phrase – has a considerable appeal, especially perhaps to the young.

Second, the market has changed in another significant way. It is now world-wide. Publishers and authors are conscious of the market for English language books in the developing countries of the Commonwealth, and of the opportunities for selling foreign rights. This makes a novelist like Rushdie who makes use of, and appeals to, other cultural traditions attractive to a publisher: though the reception accorded *The Satanic Verses* (1988) in Islamic countries may persuade publishers in the future to look more closely at the cultures with which such novels engage themselves.

This new awareness of a transnational market does not mean that publishers will necessarily shun novels which are very English (or Scottish, Irish or Welsh) because such books may sometimes appeal to a much wider readership as representative examples of their native culture. But it does mean that novels which draw from more than one culture, which have a cosmopolitan or transnational tone, may have a better chance of selling world-wide. Boyd's most recent novel, *The New Confessions*, moves through half a century of modern history and the settings include Scotland, England, France, Germany, the United States, Mexico and a Mediterranean island.

I am not suggesting that such a novel is tailored to an international market. Novelists are themselves products of their times and their society. If they appeal to a world-wide market, it is because they belong to such a market themselves. They belong, like their readers, to the world of the charge card and the international airport, a world where people are equally at home in a hamburger joint and an ethnic restaurant, where a Czech novelist like Kundera or a Peruvian one like Vargas Llosa seems to speak as directly to them as another English writer, a world where for the first time in history the writer may truthfully say: 'nihil humanum alienum est' ('Nothing human is foreign to me.'). It is impossible that such considerations should not influence the way they write themselves. To be modern is no longer to be modernist, but it is to be international.

2

A personal voice: Anthony Powell, Graham Greene, Iris Murdoch, Muriel Spark, Kingsley Amis

The most ambitious venture in post-war English fiction was brought to a triumphant conclusion in 1975. This was Anthony Powell's novel in twelve volumes, *A Dance to the Music of Time*. An unfolding of English upper-class and upper-Bohemian life, extending over more than forty years in time (and twenty-five years in the writing), it is too subtle, contrived and self-aware to be described as a *roman-fleuve*. No English novelist has matched Powell's ability to achieve an intricate intertwining of art and reality. The critic John Bayley has remarked that 'nothing shows the complete originality of Powell's technique more than the way his fiction imitates memoir, and almost in a double sense, like a *trompe-l'oeil* painting', so that the novel becomes 'an anecdote arranging itself in the elaborate composition of a picture'.

A harsher note, at times even brutal, and certainly sombre, was struck in the last two volumes, *Temporary Kings* (1973) and *Hearing Secret Harmonies* (1975). No doubt this was partly in response to changes in public morality which had afforded greater freedom to the writer, but the darker mood of these last volumes was principally determined by the inner dynamic of the whole series of novels in which characters are revealed as moving figures responding involuntarily to the mysterious music which compels them to perform intricate measures in the dance of life, according to a pattern which they neither will nor understand. So, in these last two books, which crown the series, Widmerpool, the comic, yet sinister figure who has tried to shape his life by the exercise of the will, disregarding in the process those claims of affection and sensibility which alone make life tolerable, rushes towards destruction, impelled by forces over which he has lost all control, and ultimately conquered by the more powerful will of the young Scorpio Murtlock.

Powell's achievement, unmatched by any contemporary, and indeed unique in the English novel since Henry James, was to render social reality convincing, in a rich expressive prose, while at the same time revealing the inadequacy of any attempt to understand human nature, and the human condition, only in such terms. Adroit in his deployment of factual detail, the accumulation of which makes every page ring true to life, scenes of social, army and business life all being presented with fidelity to common experience, Powell nevertheless, by the vividness of his imaginative perception, bathes the world he has called into being in the golden light of timeless myth. At its simplest level, this is the personal myth – the view of self – which each of us forms and which, if maintained, enables us to get satisfactorily, or at least tolerably, through life. But at a more profound level all his characters are seen to be enacting certain symbiotic roles in the lives of others, and hence in the reader's imagination also.

One of the most difficult of the novelist's tasks is to make those characters whom he has called into being with a few strokes of the pen achieve a semblance of autonomous life; and it is Powell's peculiar and double triumph to have brought this off, while at the same time suggesting to us that we all take on alternative lives in the minds of others, and that indeed the whole of experience may be a dream dreamed by some Great Unknown. The Spanish philosopher Jose Ortega y Gasset asked whether 'human life in its most human dimension was not a work of fiction. Is man a sort of novelist of himself?' This is the experience of Powell's characters, or rather perhaps it is the experience we have when reading of them. He contrives to make them more real than people we know – more real because they are presented with an authority we do not encounter in 'real' life – while reminding us that they are only so because he has imagined them. Like Pirandello, he 'pretends that the familiar parlour is not real as a photograph, but a stage containing many realities'. Yet he never sacrifices common sense. His myth is always an alternative interpretation, not forced on the reader.

Powell has tackled, more effectively than any other writer of our time, the essential problem of the novelist: how to achieve a balance between what he sees out of the window and what goes on in his head. Only those who strike such a balance can convince us that their view of life is both valid and interesting.

He has another attribute, the possession or lack of which is one useful test of a writer's quality: the unmistakable personal voice. The writer who lacks this may have many virtues, but is likely to be forgotten because a common voice suggests common observation.

The individual voice is perhaps the only quality which Graham Greene, Iris Murdoch, Muriel Spark and Kingsley Amis share. (It is something which neither Golding nor Burgess has.) They may be considered, with Powell, to constitute the senior quintet among post-war novelists who are still writing. All have a body of work to their credit which is impressively coherent.

Obviously by far the greater part of Greene's work falls outside the period under review. Inasmuch as there has been little change in either his manner or matter, it might seem superfluous to dwell on him here. However, two of the books which he has published since 1970 are among his finest. They are also contemporary in theme. *The Honorary Consul* (1973), set in Argentina, deals in subtle and penetrating fashion with the origins and morality of political terrorism. It is his wisest and most tender novel, which may be seen as the culmination of his life's work, but also as going beyond anything else he has written. Its theme is expressed in the epigraph, taken from Hardy: 'All things merge into one another – good into evil, generosity into justice, religion into politics.' Whereas the lonely and perturbed heroes of earlier Greene experience pity as something corrupting, now, in a sense that Hardy would have recognized, pity is revealed as the emotion which makes life tolerable. There is no condescension in this pity, for Charley Fortnum, the weak and foolish hero who has nevertheless survived, finds himself extending pity to the young wife who has cuckolded him, and knows that the emotion springs from his own sense of unworthiness. So: 'in an affair of this kind it was the right thing to lie. He felt a sense of immense relief. It was as though, after what seemed an interminable time of anxious waiting in the ante-room of death, someone came to him with the good news he had never expected to hear. Someone he loved would survive. He realized that never before had she been as close to him as she was now.'

Graham Greene

Pity is the dominant note in *The Human Factor* (1978) also. Superficially this novel of the Secret Service may seem a slighter thing, for in it Greene plays again with genre fiction and employs many of the tricks of sleight of hand that characterize the thriller. But the heart of the novel is of the utmost seriousness: Castle, the hero, is led to justified treachery by his experience of pity and love. It is a bleak novel, with an ending that is as miserable as anything Greene has written. His characters are at the mercy of malign forces as far beyond their understanding as their control; and yet at the end one is left with a conviction of the strength and durability of love and pity.

A great writer's achievement is more that the sum of individual novels. Greene's is a world where men are heroes without hope, continually betrayed to self-destruction by whatever is best in themselves. Profoundly conscious of the fragility of civilization and the corruptibility of the heart, Greene is nevertheless an affirmative writer. It is said that he has been denied the Nobel Prize because certain members of the Swedish Academy do not believe his work is 'of an idealistic tendency', which the conditions of the prize stipulate as a necessary qualification. Yet what can be more idealistic than his affirmation of the value of love and pity in a world given over to fraud and violence?

Murdoch, Spark and Amis all published their first novels in the middle 1950s, and half their career therefore falls within my period. Such a division is insignificant, for the work of all three displays a characteristic unity. This does not mean that there has been no development; rather that such development has taken place within a pattern already formed by their early work. They have all been regarded as important novelists from the start, though all have had their detractors.

Murdoch is of the three the easiest to characterize and the hardest to assess. Her novels are markedly individual. She has declared her allegiance to the large realistic tradition of the nineteenth-century novel, specifically English and Russian. She takes great care to place her carefully described characters in a precise social setting, to give them a history and family relationships. At the same time her intricate and extravagant plots, which combine comedy with elements of the grotesque

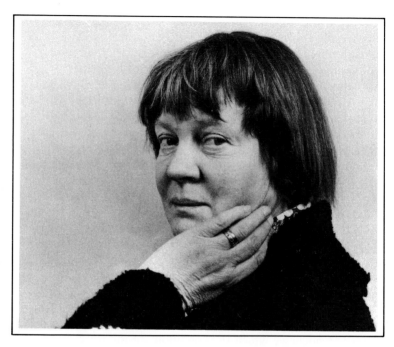

Iris Murdoch

and the macabre, are patterned in a manner wholly artificial. They conform habitually to arbitrarily determined symbolic structures. Likewise her dialogue, though both witty and imaginative, is such as never issued from human mouth; it is as if the reader is being made privy to what her characters might say if they gave verbal expression to what they feel, rather than to what they would say in a particular situation.

Admirers have compared her novels to the late plays of Shakespeare, and the comparison holds good to this extent: that she is willing to mix comedy with melodrama, and to present the improbable and impossible with assurance and without explanation, in order to allow her to explore matters of great importance, such as the nature of good and evil, the temptations of religion and magic, and the effects of sexuality on individual and social life. She writes novels in which repressions are brought to the surface and made words. Because she is not afraid to topple into absurdity, as she does at moments in every novel, her prose losing its precision and becoming exaggerated and bombastic, she is also capable of moments of illuminating insight. In her intellectual rigour and her willingness to write about the most intense emotions in a comic mode, she may be seen as the successor to Ivy Compton-Burnett, whom she also resembles in the deliberate melodrama of her plotting. On the other hand, her exact, even meticulous, description of the surface of life, of the appearance of her characters, their houses, clothes, furnishings and meals, would seem to make her a realist even in the manner of Arnold Bennett.

Muriel Spark resembles her in the willingness to mix realism with an awareness of a dimension of experience beyond what is normally conveyed by that word. Where Murdoch goes for amplitude, however, Spark prefers economy. Her novels represent a distillation of experience; she has always remained true to her sense that 'everything happens to an artist; time is always redeemed, nothing is lost, and wonders never cease' (*Loitering with Intent*, 1981). Her novels are notable not for their fidelity to life, nor for an attempt to impose patterns on experience, but rather for their awareness of that strange substance whence patterns are formed. Inasmuch as the novelist's problem is to effect the perfect marriage between manner and matter, so that the novel satisfies as an aesthetic object, while at the same time permitting the elaboration of discussible themes, then she succeeds time and again.

Nowhere is this more evident than in *The Only Problem* (1984). The subject might seem too large for fiction, for it is that posed in *The Book of Job*: 'how can an omnipotent and benevolent Creator permit the unspeakable sufferings of the world?' Conversely, this short novel might seem too slight for its subject. But *Job* itself is a short book, and as Spark makes her hero Harvey Gotham observe, in a judgement that might be applied to the whole body of her fiction (or at least to its spirit): 'moving passages about for no other reason than that they are more logical is no good for the *Book of Job*. It doesn't make it come clear. *The Book of Job* will never come clear. It doesn't matter. It's a poem.'

Acceptance of the fundamentally mysterious nature of life is crucial to an appreciation of Spark. Truth is beyond reason, its recognition an act of faith. But experience itself cannot be bounded by reason either. Human nature is contrary, and its remorseless selfishness always threatens to destroy the fabric which alone can sustain it. Spark's art is founded on paradox. The manner is inconsequential, but no modern writer has a clearer sense of the ineluctable nature of consequence. She has said that her narrative model is to be found in the Border Ballads, where one thing happens and then another, without explanation. Yet no one has a more intrusive authorial voice, setting us right, warning, advising, or choosing to mislead. She can write of the gravest matters in the lightest, even most frivolous, of tones, and then remind us that a thoughtless and apparently unimportant action can have the most appalling consequence, and be, in fact, a monstrous sin.

Kingsley Amis is a moralist too, and one whose career presents us with certain paradoxes. No writer has spoken more scornfully of experiment – or none since Waugh – and yet, though dismissive of linguistic experiment, he has succumbed several times to the temptation to experiment with themes, even with reality. He has, for instance, written novels set in the future (*Russian Hide-and-Seek*, 1980) and in an imaginary parallel or alternative time-scheme (*The Alteration*, 1976). Yet his best novels are faithful to one of the central traditions of the English novel: social comedy.

His work has always been attacked by critics who dislike

its social–political tone. In the days when he was considered an 'Angry Young Man', he was thought representative of a new philistinism: Somerset Maugham dismissed him, his characters, and other novelists who were given the same label, as 'scum'. More recently Amis has been arraigned for right-wing opinions and alleged misogyny. This last accusation is strange, for he is among the comparatively few English novelists whose heroes are almost all heterosexual and unable to exist happily without the company of women. Of course they are frequently mystified and irritated by women also, but female novelists whose heroines find men similarly puzzling and annoying are not usually charged with being hostile to the other sex.

Amis has always been an enemy of cant from whatever source it emanates. He has a marvellous ear for insincerity and diagnoses pretention with happy accuracy. He is a master of the comic set-piece. He is concerned, in his best novels, with the way we live now, and his true master is Fielding. Like Fielding he places his heroes in situations where desire is at odds with duty. In *Difficulties with Girls* (1988) the debt to Fielding is directly acknowledged: a marked copy of *Tom Jones* plays a significant part in the climactic scene; Patrick Standish and his wife Jenny are essentially the Fielding hero and heroine in modern dress.

His most recent novels, *Stanley and the Women* (1984), *The Old Devils* (1986) and *Difficulties with Girls*, have revealed qualities not apparent in his earlier fiction. Though he retains his abrupt sense of comic discrepancy, there has been a new tenderness and depth of understanding. This was especially apparent in the portrayal of relations between Stanley and his mentally disturbed son. Though Stanley was clumsy and imperceptive in other areas of life, in this relationship Amis for the first time depicted love convincingly. Desire and lust had been frequent enough in his novels, but not a love which could deny or transcend self. It was a pointer towards the mature and subtle treatment of Jenny's love for Patrick in *Difficulties with Girls* and the sensitive treatment of old age in *The Old Devils*.

Having moved uncertainly through the 1970s, Amis has therefore burst into new flower in the 1980s. These last three novels have finally established him as a master of his generation, and the foremost example in our time of the English tradition of comic realism.

3

The moral imperative: A. S. Byatt, Margaret Drabble, Stanley Middleton, David Storey, Stan Barstow, Alan Sillitoe, William McIlvanney, James Kelman, Alasdair Gray, Iain Crichton Smith

There has long been a division in the English novel between the provincial and the metropolitan. It was made critically respectable by the influential Cambridge teacher and critic F. R. Leavis. His contempt for Bloomsbury and for the reviewing standards of the London press, for everything that he characterized as dilettante and élitist, encouraged admiration for those qualities which seemed to stand in permanent opposition to what he disliked: and these he found represented in the puritan culture of the English provinces. Leavis was in fact every bit as élitist as those he denounced, but his élite was moral and intellectual, not social.

His teaching remains an important influence on the contemporary English novel. A clear example is offered by the novels of A. S. Byatt: *The Virgin in the Garden* (1978) and *Still Life* (1985), the first two volumes of a planned quartet. Uncommonly interesting, at least in so far as they raise matters for discussion and offer a fictional social history of England from the early 1950s, these novels dramatize the distinction between the provinces and the metropolis, and another distinction, becoming more apparent over the whole period in which they are set, between traditional ideas of high culture and the mass culture which threatens to destroy inherited and admirable ways of living and modes of experience.

So, for instance, Byatt observes that Alexander Wedderburn (a poet and dramatist) 'had come to London as successful writers did, or successful characters at the end of those exploratory novels which analysed and celebrated working-class values and virtues in the North, whose authors and heroes hurried down as fast as they could to the busy capital. The Pooles too were very deliberately leaving the provinces, making themselves metropolitan. They had left almost everything behind – the three-piece suite, the Wilton carpets, the glass-fronted bookcase, the family silver. Elinor Poole said to Alexander that the exciting thing was that the flat was *flat*, the rooms, all in a row, just rooms. You could sleep or eat in any or all of them . . . .'

A settled way of life has been replaced by a provisional existence which will be altered in accordance with changing fashions. With his friend Poole, Alexander speaks 'of Dr Leavis and the common pursuit of true judgement, of how they would miss the Yorkshire moors, of the possible future use of television in education'. But, in this provisional society, Byatt asks, is 'the common pursuit of true judgement' still possible?

It is the seriousness of Byatt's approach which is attractive, her conviction that one purpose of fiction is still to teach us how to live, by refining our perceptions and deepening our understanding of human nature and society. She is too intelligent to set up crude opposites, to find virtue exclusively in one way of life, but, while admitting the attractions of the new, she allows us to see where it is defective; and so sets the conditions for a criticism of social change. She is a writer whose capacity to interest is greater than her ability to delight. She is didactic and long-winded; she has little sense of structure and no elegance. But her novels are nevertheless impressive, discussible objects, invaluable to an understanding of English life and culture.

She herself, born in Yorkshire, educated there and at Cambridge, a university that had always seemed to set provincial worth against the metropolitan glitter of Oxford, has gravitated to London, like the heroes of those Northern novels to which she refers. So has her sister Margaret Drabble, another novelist whose best work concerns itself with the divisions in English life, and with a critical examination of new directions being taken by English society. Drabble's early novels established her as the representative voice of educated women of her generation. To some extent she has remained this, but her work has become much more ambitious, as it has moved away from the personal–anecdotal novels with which she made her name. Her true subject now is the moral condition of England.

She tackles this with zest and virtuosity in her most recent, and most ambitious, novel, *The Radiant Way* (1987). It opens brilliantly. Liz Headland, a successful psychotherapist, is giving a New Year's party to usher in the 1980s. At the same time she is celebrating twenty-one years of marriage to Charles, a television producer. The duration of their marriage is 'unique in their circle of acquaintance. Battle and bloodshed and betrayal lay behind them, and now they met peacefully in this large house, and slept peacefully in their separate rooms, and met at week-ends over the marmalade, and would continue to do so until Charles's new appointment took him, in a couple of months, to New York.' Liz congratulates herself on their achievement in language which suggests to the reader that her complacency is about to be shattered, that it is not as easy as she supposes to solve the problems of modern living. The party, handled with an assurance that is both scintillating and significant, reveals the extent of her self-deception. Her acute perceptions are not so acute. She has misunderstood her own life.

It is a weakness of the novel that this misunderstanding is not apparently intended to discredit her as a guide to the way we live now. In fact her response to the contemporary world is confused. Despite this, *The Radiant Way* is an unusually persuasive novel. It celebrates the power of friendship and it is animated by Drabble's awareness of objects – landscape, food and drink – by her sense of the surging metropolis and the cold cities of the North. Yet it is also angry, sombre and pessimistic. Her analysis of contemporary England is harsh. She is alarmed by the sense that social obligation is being supplanted by compulsion and selfishness. Her puritanism is offended by the new individualism which flaunts wealth, is thrilled by power, and has no respect for what should bind people together. Despite the anger, she is a sufficiently subtle moralist to realize that this is, in part, the consequence of what people like herself, and those characters she admires, have successfully demanded: that is, the freedom to live their own way, by standards they have chosen for themselves. Moreover, she knows that right is rarely concentrated on one side. In a scene at the end of the novel, Liz is having dinner with her

Margaret Drabble

friends Alix and Esther; they discover that the police have surrounded the house, intending to arrest a young man on the top floor. Liz is hostile to the police; she calls them 'a bloody disgrace . . . thick as two planks . . . incompetent fools'; she says 'perhaps they're hoping he will take all three of us hostage and they can have a big shoot-out. They like that kind of thing'. But Alix argues the cause of the police: 'it wasn't their fault if they had learned confrontation, their position in urban society was increasingly untenable'.

The strength of Drabble's fiction rests in its nineteenth-century seriousness. She never doubts the importance of the social world in which we live and which she seeks to reflect. Like Byatt, she never doubts that the novel has a part to play in deepening and refining our understanding of society. She cares passionately about the way we live, and credits her readers with a similarly intense concern. If her novels sometimes lack imaginative illumination, for which she tries to compensate by writing in a torrential style, in which adjectives and tautologies are heaped up with all the exuberance of a Victorian painter assembling fruit, vegetables and the carcasses of game-birds for a still-life painting, she has a concomitant virtue: she never takes refuge from facts in elaborate fantasy. It is always here and now in her world; she has a respect for physical reality that is admirable and invigorating.

So has Stanley Middleton. He is the outstanding novelist of Middle England, greatly admired by Byatt who has written that his 'is a world of questing morality, without the sanction of religious injunction, upheld only by decency'. This is indeed the world in which all these writers live. It is perhaps the reward of a provincial upbringing in a society where 'smart' was not an admiring adjective, and where 'duty' was still presented as a moral imperative.

Middleton is the Cézanne of the modern English novel, achieving extraordinary effects with apparently the most ordinary of materials. He works at the same subject again and again, and its matter is never in itself striking or remarkable. His novels are all set in the Midlands and his characters are drawn from the middle classes: schoolmasters, solicitors, businessmen, whose roots are generally to be found in a narrow chapel-going culture, which has in the course of time lost its religious element without surrendering its ethical content. Typically, his plot poses a complex moral problem: we find marriages at breaking-point, people having to come to terms with retirement, bereavement or estrangement. 'He works', Byatt observes, 'on the borders between people where the nature of the self of the other is a mystery and a blank'.

In his later novels, like 'The Daysman', 'An After-Dinner Sleep' and 'Recovery', his mastery is so assured that he in fact dispenses with 'plot' in the formal sense of the term. Instead he fastens on the haphazard nature of life. There is of course a story, but there is a story as there is one in ordinary experience. One thing succeeds another, and there is no satisfactory shape to events. To write a novel in this way is to take a great risk, for no work of art can dispense with form. The movement in a Middleton novel is internal. It is his characters' state of mind and spirit which is important, and it is by his deployment of feeling rather than incident that he contrives to give his work an aesthetically, and therefore morally, satisfying pattern. His characters are committed to a moral obstacle course, by means of which they learn, or learn again, how to go on living in the right way. Part of the strain imposed on them comes from their realization that in the modern world they have to make their own code of decent behaviour.

Middleton works tentatively, his prose echoing his characters' uncertainties and divagations. His is always an exploratory art. The sense of felt life is one of his qualities: he is admirable in the evocation of place, weather, mood, and in the isolation of significant moments in experience. He is also consistently interesting. This sounds a weak adjective of praise; yet the ability to be interesting, to make what happens to the characters he has imagined seem to matter to the reader, is not the least of the novelist's required talents. Indeed it is a fundamental one: if the writer does not possess it, all his other gifts may go for nothing.

On the whole, the people in Middleton's novels are decent, well-meaning, unremarkable; they really are the sort of people we might have as neighbours. Most of them try to be good, to be pleasant; they could even be called nice. Their ordinariness is a mark of the author's ambition. It is easier to create wild, flamboyant and extraordinary characters; the portrayal of evil is always a temptation to the writer because it is more dramatic than good. Middleton, however, brings to the depiction of ordinary humdrum undramatic life the high seriousness which less subtle and understanding writers can bring only to awful and extraordinary events.

David Storey and Stan Barstow deal more often with working-class life. This distinguishes them from Byatt, Drabble and Middleton, whom however they resemble in that they take the reality of everyday social experience as their starting-point, never forgetting the influence that the demands of society and the human environment exert on the individual.

Storey won the Booker Prize in 1976 with *Saville*, a large and powerful book set in a south Yorkshire mining village. The influence of D. H. Lawrence on his fiction is obvious: a characteristic theme, as for instance in *The Prodigal Child* (1982), is that of a young man educated out of his class, subsequently at home neither in the new world he has entered nor in the old one from which he has been torn. His dislocation and alienation allow Storey to subject both parts of society to a penetrating, and frequently, disturbing analysis. As the son of a miner himself, then educated at the Slade School of Art, Storey's grasp of this situation, itself a common feature of post-war Britain, is authentic. His works are not autobiographical, but their emotion evidently derives from personal experience. Though his debt to Lawrence is considerable, there is one important difference between them. Whereas Lawrence's novels give the impression of being spontaneous outpourings of irrepressible feeling, Storey's are carefully wrought, the prose often congested. The evidence of thought and preparation can be seen in his treatment of his characters; his judgement of where they stand is always trustworthy.

Stan Barstow is one of these novelists, like Alan Sillitoe and John Braine, cursed by an early success that the public delights to remember while neglecting the author's more interesting mature novels. He is a writer who prefers straightforward narrative: his most recent novel, with the ironic title *B-Movie* (1987), is the story of a murder committed by a young man in the course of robbing a jeweller's shop, and of his arrest while on holiday in Blackpool. Set in the post-war years, with the events seen mostly through the eyes of the murderer's friend, it allies period charm to emotional subtlety; it is like the work of a more tender-hearted Simenon. Barstow's strength rests in the honesty with which he explores the way people feel. He is a writer you can trust, for he falsifies nothing, is never showy. His use of detail is perceptive, exact and economical, and his books are warm and loving, without pretending that life itself is all warmth and love. His response to experience is affirmative. His best book is perhaps *Just You Wait and See* (1986). This study of a family during the Second World War is traditional in style, and traditional also in its theme, which is indeed that of all Jane Austen's novels: whom should the heroine marry? Barstow never forgets that in a mature and decent society personal relations are the serious business of life; all the more significantly so in a community which lacks the leisure that might allow its members to make a cult of them.

Alan Sillitoe shares many virtues with Barstow, though he is more self-consciously literary. His early novels, especially the first, *Saturday Night and Sunday Morning* (1958), were praised as examples of working-class realism, but Sillitoe has never been content to repeat himself or to be restricted by the categorization which is the habit of idle reviewers. In fact his talent has always been evocative rather than mimetic. He writes with most feeling of the strange half-urban, half-rural world of the Nottinghamshire coalfield, memorably in the autobiographical *Raw Material* (1972); but he is a good example of the truth that a writer's subject is always to some extent accidental, the result of what life has thrown in his way; what matters is the talent he brings to it. Sillitoe, with his ability to look hard at experience, and then transform it into fiction and a prose that is always alert to nuances, is a very fine novelist, whose work is distinguished by a poetic sense of unrealized possibilities.

William McIlvanney also comes from a mining background. The Ayrshire coalfields are the setting for his best novel *Docherty* (1975). He differs from Storey and Sillitoe, however, in that, himself of Irish extraction but born and brought up in the west of Scotland, he is aware of a much richer historical culture of which his characters have been deprived. *Docherty* is, in a sense, a historical novel, for it covers the first quarter of the century. Its hero, Tam Docherty, is a miner who incarnates working-class virtue, but who, unlike the fathers in Lawrence's novels, is eager that his sons should escape the life he has been compelled, by economic circumstance, to lead. When his fourth child, Conn, is born, he cries: 'he'll never be ready for the pits. No' this wan. He'll howk wi' his heid. Fur ideas . . . Ah'm pittin his name doon fur Prime Minister. First thing in the morning.' The hope is vain: Tam 'had fathered four children and all he had ever been able to give them was their personal set of shackles'. The novel is simultaneously a protest and a celebration: a protest against an economic system that denies men their native dignity, and a celebration of those who refuse to accept that denial. It is a noble and generous book, though marred by a relish of violence which borders on the sentimental in that it is admired without thought of its consequences: this has disfigured McIlvanney's subsequent work, especially *The Big Man* (1985).

McIlvanney is only one of a number of writers, many like him from the west, who have made the last two decades a rich period in the history of the Scottish novel. More ambitious than McIlvanney is James Kelman, a writer of unsparing truthfulness. In *The Bus-Conductor Hines* (1983), he achieves authority as a result of his determination to present the detail of a limited, indeed deprived, life honestly. Kelman writes in an unpretentious demotic; the dialogue faithfully, yet imaginatively, reproducing the rhythms of working-class Scots speech, necessarily stylized, poses problems for English readers. But he is a writer who merits close attention. He is an urban novelist, his territory the grim housing-schemes on the periphery of Glasgow. The drab existences he describes are as far from metropolitan glitter as you can get. No other British novelist of the last twenty years has looked more closely, with a sympathy that does not slide into sentimentality, at the way the poor are compelled to live. To ignore Kelman is to ignore those areas of modern life where society fails its members.

Kelman has been closely associated with Alasdair Gray. This might seem an accident of friendship, which has led them to publish a joint collection of stories, *Lean Tales* (along with Agnes Owen) (1985), rather than an indication of anything they have in common as writers, for, at first sight, Gray appears to be as much of a fantasist as Kelman is a realist. Certainly Gray's shorter fiction, *Unlikely Stories, Mostly* (1983) are self-conscious, artificial, mannered, while two of the four parts of his most substantial work, *Lanark* (1981), are set in an imaginary netherworld deriving equally, it might seem, from Kafka and science fiction. Nevertheless appearances are deceptive here: these parts encapsulate a naturalistic autobiographical novel about growing up in Glasgow, and indeed all Gray's work, however decorative its façade, grows from the roots of his own experience: he is a fantasist whose food is social reality. *Lanark* is a novel of remarkable structural ambition, playful in a post-modernist mode; yet its peculiar strength derives from its close relation to everyday life in Glasgow. Without this anchor it would float into self-indulgent limbo. The nature of Gray's talent is made still clearer in *1982, Janine*. A great part of this work consists of the masturbatory fantasies of the chief character, in whose mind indeed the whole novel takes place. But these fantasies are his response to the social pressures to which he has been subjected; at its heart the novel is as much a cry of protest against everything in modern urban life which stultifies personality, and denies the expression of generous impulses, as Kelman's novels more evidently are.

The failure to which Iain Crichton Smith directs our attention is also primarily moral. A Gaelic speaker and a poet, Crichton Smith finds his characteristic subjects on the geographical periphery of Britain. He writes of small communities where a traditional way of life is in decay, and where nothing valuable has been found to replace it. A deceptively simple writer, Crichton Smith is aware of the narrowness of that old way of life, imposed by a fierce, cold, frequently life-denying religion, which he cannot admire. Yet at the same time, in, for instance, *A Field Full of Folk* (1982), he shows how the loss of old moral certainties and the decline of prescriptive religion leave people apparently at the mercy of events which they can neither comprehend nor control. The central figures in his novels commonly experience a sense of alienation; they are compelled to try to make sense of a broken pattern. Destruction threatens them; the heroes of *The Search* (1983), set in Australia, and of *In the Middle of the Wood* (1987) both suffer a nervous breakdown. Crichton Smith's view of life is not, however, unremittingly bleak. Triumph is possible. The Reverend Peter Murchison in *A Field Full of Folk*, though assailed by loss of faith and stricken with cancer, nevertheless concludes that 'we are really free to live and die. If it were not so we would have been told. Don't look for the kingdom of God elsewhere. The kingdom of God is all around you. Even in the eyes of this grieving woman, even in her helpless curses, the chain stretches to infinity.'

4

Politics and the novel: Doris Lessing, Nadine Gordimer, Brian Moore, William Trevor, V. S. Naipaul, Ruth Prawer Jhabvala, Piers Paul Read, Fay Weldon

The strengths of the novels discussed in the last chapter, provincial, or Scottish, generally thirled to a sort of naturalism, are evident; their weaknesses equally so. Though they need not, as Drabble shows, eschew politics, and though indeed all these novels, in one way or another, reflect an awareness of the part played by politics in the formation of a culture, nevertheless concerned with characters who are, in political terms, more acted upon than acting, the authors of such novels tend not to concern themselves with the problem of power except in a narrow familial sphere. These novels do not deal with a world where men kill each other on account of what they believe. They treat of a society uninterested in ideology. (Gray might seem an exception to this generalization.)

For this reason such novels can seem parochial and even escapist to writers and readers from other cultures in which politics remains a matter of life and death, rather than the distribution of perquisites and benefits. Terrorism, the police state, armed rebellion are not themes that commend themselves to writers like Middleton, Byatt and Barstow. Drabble flirts with violent matter in, for instance, *Jerusalem the Golden* (1976); but her engagement scarcely goes deeper than dinner-party conversation.

Yet there are other traditions in the English-language novel, even if those who follow them are themselves often the products of other cultures: they may be termed the heirs of Conrad, the Polish author of the greatest corpus of political fiction written in English since Sir Walter Scott. No one could, for instance, accuse Doris Lessing or Nadine Gordimer of failing to examine the nature of politics and the consequences

Doris Lessing *(Photograph © Miriam Berkley)*

of political action. Lessing, brought up in Southern Rhodesia, sometime member of the Communist Party, has always been keenly aware of the effect of economic forces on ideology. She attacked the colour bar, long before it was fashionable to do so, and may be regarded as one of the literary pioneers of the Women's Movement. Her best work was done before the period under review, which indeed she chiefly occupied with a five-volume work *The Canopus in Argos Archives* (1979–83). These science fiction novels revealed considerable power of invention, marred by the arbitrary freedom and imaginative, as distinct from fanciful, inertia characteristic of the genre. Nevertheless, her influence has been profound.

Nadine Gordimer's work is almost entirely concerned with the political situation of her native South Africa. She is a passionate enemy of apartheid whose writing never forsakes the complexities of fiction for the easier simplicities of journalism that are the temptation for the political novelist. She has written at least three remarkable novels: *The Conservationist* (1974), a triumph of style in which a rich man tries in self-interest to challenge, and arrest, the movement of history; *Burger's Daughter* (1979), the personal and political story of a girl whose Communist father died in a South African prison; and *July's People* (1981), set in the future when South Africa has crumbled into civil war, and a white family have become dependent, in a wholly new way, on their black servants. Gordimer's novels are distinguished by the rich expressiveness of her prose and by her ability to combine political passion with moral discrimination and compassion for those caught in the trap of history.

Other South African novelists such as J. M. Coetzee and Christopher Hope have found material in the stark injustices of their native land. Writers are formed by the experience of their environment as much as by their own temperament and native gift of imagination. South African novelists are granted material such as novelists formed in more humane political cultures must seek out.

Irish writers, conscious of the troubled history of their country's struggle for independence and by the continuing sharp and cruel divisions between Catholic and Protestant in the North, cannot avoid acquiring a body of experience comparable to the South African. This is apparent in the work of Brian Moore, William Trevor, Jennifer Johnston and younger writers like Bernand MacLaverty and Neil Jordan.

Moore has attained international celebrity, and often displays an international range of subject-matter, even sometimes a blandness of tone, without ever quite losing the distinctive Irish identity apparent in early Belfast novels like *The Lonely Passion of Judith Hearne* (1955) and *The Emperor of Ice-Cream* (1965); the second of these deals with IRA activities at the beginning of the Second World War. Since then his work has been marked by its variety of subject-matter, culminating in the remarkable *Black Robe* (1984), a historical novel about Jesuit missionaries in seventeenth-century Canada, captured, tortured and martyred by Indian tribes. Yet even this novel in which the drama arises from the clash of uncomprehending cultures may be seen to have its roots in his Irish experience.

This is all the more true of *The Colour of Blood* (1987). Masterly in its economy, it is set in an unnamed Eastern European country, which every reader will identify as Poland. The chief character is a cardinal whose willingness to co-operate with the Communist authorities, whom he nevertheless condemns, has aroused the anger of Catholic–Nationalist zealots. They kidnap him, hoping to provoke a crisis, since it will be assumed that he has been arrested by the state. Yet, though the atmosphere of Eastern Europe is convincingly evoked, this is still, in Moore's words, 'the novel I have always wanted to write about Ireland'.

How can this be? In the last chapter, the Cardinal tells his flock that we live under

the tyranny of an age when religious beliefs have become inextricably entwined with political hatreds. . . . I have allowed my people to come to the brink of violence, to a confusion between the wrongs that have been done to us and the wrongs that some among us now advocate we do in return. I beg you to think of the deaths of others. Remember, the tyrant and the terrorist have that in common. They do not think of those deaths.

The colour of blood is the same everywhere: this is the observation of a humanist who would have people no longer die for abstract words, whether in Poland, Ireland or Central

America. Moore's novels are concerned with the abuse of power. Even an apparently domestic story like *The Doctor's Wife* (1976) turns on the question of power, set in opposition to freedom. His novels are open-ended; the world beyond them presses in on his characters. They are always caught in a particular moment of history, their freedom of choice limited by historical imperatives. They cannot exist in isolation from the culture that has helped to shape them. For this reason their problems cannot be resolved in private–personal terms.

The same is true when William Trevor writes of Ireland. Trevor, possibly at his best in the short story, of which he is, along with V. S. Pritchett, the supreme master among contemporary writers, has become steadily more ambitious as a novelist. His novels set in England are generally unremarkable, *The Children of Dynmouth* (1975), for instance, not quite coming off as a study of motiveless evil. Perhaps the reason for the comparative failure of his English novels is to be found in the lack of any sense of historical urgency behind themes and characters. It is precisely this sense which makes *Fools of Fortune* (1983) and *The Silence in the Garden* (1988) so impressive. Both these novels have a long historical sweep; both present us with characters and social groups deformed by historical experience. In an ironical twist, the ruling class, the Protestant Ascendancy of Ireland, have become the victims, diminished, marginalized, spiritually impoverished by the movement of events over which they have no control. Like Moore, Trevor makes us aware of the destruction wrought by idealism. At the same time both view history as an impersonal uncontrolled force, indifferent to any moral considerations.

Like Trevor, V. S. Naipaul first seemed a minor artist of considerable charm. Like him he has developed into something more formidable. Like Moore he is ready to take the deepest themes of the modern world as his subject. He has an ambition which is extreme. His experience of the way men behave in the world today is expressed in novels which are sombre, . melancholy, and pessimistic. He is a writer who sees in the fractured cultures of the twentieth century the opportunity for everything that is vile, cruel and barbaric to rise to the surface. The destruction of settled political and cultural order has bred moral disorder; we suffer its consequences, and find no sure refuge. *Guerrillas* (1975), a story of political and sexual violence in the emergent Caribbean, ends with a sado-masochistic murder. *A Bend in the River* (1979) charts the progress of a recently independent Central African state through a group of varied characters. Again the tone is pessimistic: violent change, however well intentioned, tears man from his inherited culture, and leaves him wandering in a dangerous waste land.

His most recent novel, *The Enigma of Arrival* (1987), is also his most personal. It is indeed a long autobiographical meditation in fictional form on Naipaul's own relations with England and the loss of permanence. The title is taken from a painting by the Italian master Giorgio di Chirico, itself enigmatic and disturbing: a ship, sail billowing, disappears into the distance. Two cloaked figures stand before a blank red wall. Part of a chess board stretches before them. Behind rises a round pillared tower on which the light falls, revealing nothing. The figures are condemned, there can be no doubt, to sojourn in the city, play out the game to which they have been committed, and of which they are ignorant. It is a metaphor for Naipaul's view of our condition. The modern world has arrived at a point where we are all immigrants, ignorant of what is expected of us.

In an essay on Conrad, the novelist whom he most often echoes, whose heir he, in a sense, very clearly is, Naipaul wrote:

the novel as a form no longer carries conviction. Experimentation, not aimed at the real difficulties (which are that 'the great societies that produced the great novels have cracked') has corrupted response. . . . The novelist, like the painter, no longer recognizes his interpretive function; he seeks to go beyond it, and his audience diminishes. And so the world we inhabit, which is always new, goes by unexamined, made ordinary by the camera, unmediated on; and there is no one to awaken the sense of true wonder. That is perhaps a fair definition of the novelist's purpose, in all ages.

Naipaul is faithful to this purpose, nowhere more so than in *The Enigma of Arrival*. It is a book full of a sense of wonder, as the author meditates on the nature of the English landscape in which he has settled and the English people by whom he is surrounded. It is the story of how Naipaul has made himself,

V. S. Naipaul

of how he has come to terms with his own history of shattered culture. 'It came to me', he wrote in that same essay on Conrad, 'that the great novelists wrote about highly organized societies. I had no such society; I couldn't share the assumptions of the writers; I didn't see my world reflected in theirs. My colonial world was more mixed and secondhand, and more restricted.' It was out of that experience that he wrote to make himself.

Now, in a world itself mixed, second-hand and restricted, in a world in which all cultures are seen to be incomplete, disorganized by the influence of other ones, Naipaul is a writer who can be taken as a guide. He has meditated on his personal experience, which is more like that of the rest of us than he could have imagined possible as a young man. It is because of this that he speaks with rare authority. He draws attention to a phrase of Conrad's: 'the exasperated vanity of ignorance'. It is something he has identified as a characteristic of the modern world; his novels reveal it, and seek to dispel it by arousing again the sense of wonder.

Naipaul, an Indian Brahmin, born and brought up in Trinidad, has lived most of his adult life in England. He is a citizen of the world where nevertheless he finds himself a perpetual stranger. His literary culture is Western; yet he inherits another cultural tradition which was subjected by the imperialism of which his Western literary culture was the expression. He is inevitably a transnational writer, for history has made him a quintessential late-twentieth-century man, a poet of the breaking or dissolution of distinct and exclusive cultures.

Ruth Prawer Jhabvala's experience has been comparable, though very different. She was born in Germany in 1927, the daughter of a Polish Jewish lawyer. She came to England as a refugee in 1939. She married an Indian architect in 1951 and lived for most of the next quarter-century in Delhi. She moved to New York in 1975. Most of her fiction is set in India, but the principal characters are often European. *Heat and Dust*, in which she handles a double time-scheme with great success and treats with sensitive perception of love across the racial divide, won the Booker Prize in 1975. A more ambitious, if less achieved, novel is *Three Continents* (1987). It is a story of credulity, fanaticism and fraud; its theme the yearning for certainty in a world where old assumptions and codes of behaviour are no longer valid. Jhabvala works at the meeting-point of different cultures. Her strengths as a novelist are traditional; she tries to impose the order of art on the disorder from which her stories emerge. Her characters are deracinated, but her novels are fruitful because they have their roots in literary modes which are capable of perpetual renewal.

The awareness that we live in a time when nothing is certain, when all knowledge and custom have come to seem merely provisional, informs Piers Paul Read's work. Read is a rarity, a purely English novelist who is interested in ideology and whose novels arise out of his awareness of cultural disintegration and the threat to the autonomous individual posed by the modern bureaucratic state, itself a substitute for spontaneous and authentic culture. Read's characters, conscious of history, trapped in its movement, seek to free themselves by individual acts of self-assertion. Read's concerns have remained the same, but his style has changed markedly over the last twenty years. Whereas *The Junkers* (1968) was oblique, allusive, structurally complex, and adroit in its use of a narrator who only knew a small part of the story he was telling, *The Free Frenchman* (1986) was straightforward in narrative method, conventional in the use of language, structurally simple, and written from the point of view of an omniscient author. No one could read the earlier novel without realizing that the author was interested in how to employ fictional techniques; twenty years later he seemed indifferent to them, his primary concern apparently being to make his novel accessible to a wide readership. Such a development could be interpreted as evidence of a loss of ambition; yet it was perhaps much more an example of how the literary novel has moved back into the mainstream, eschewing the self-conscious experimentation that threatened to confine the reading of novels to a minority. For perhaps the most significant fact about these two novels was that they were equally ambitious in theme: *The Junkers* explored the relationship of a family of East Prussian landowners to the Nazi regime; *The Free Frenchman* unfolded with masterly and detailed confidence the story of how a divided France confronted the experience of defeat and resistance during the Second World War. In both novels Read asserted the novelist's duty to concern himself with public affairs, affirming the impossibility of writing a truthful novel about the century if the reality of history and ideology was denied or ignored. In both novels he showed how private life could be corrupted and deformed, but also justified or revitalized, by commitment to public affairs; in both he demonstrated how the characteristic English timidity in these matters narrowed the scope and diminished the authority of fiction.

In Read's novels characters are tested by a political culture which recognizes that, as the American Supreme Court judge Oliver Wendell Holmes put it, 'every society rests on the death of men'. Read would accept, as most of his English contemporaries might not, the force behind Holmes's words, which is that of an ineluctable logic: 'between two groups that want to make inconsistent kinds of world I see no remedy except force'. Though Read now writes in a plain style, he is closer in his recognition of this truth to admired Latin American writers such as Marquez and Vargas Llosa than are many who seek to imitate their style and mannerisms, but would shrink from their assumptions.

On the whole feminist fiction stops short of this sort of logic. Nevertheless the feminist novel is a political act of a seriousness which goes beyond the mild rearrangements of social relations which would satisfy a writer like Margaret Drabble. A feminist novelist like Fay Weldon is never in any doubt that the relationship between the sexes is primarily a matter of power politics; in this she is close to writers like Read and Naipaul who recognize the importance of the drive for power in human affairs. Weldon writes with a light touch that cannot disguise the clarity, indeed the ruthlessness, of her vision. Her novels, especially her masterpiece, *Praxis,* (1979) repeat Lenin's question: 'who whom?' Though her recent fiction has suffered from self-indulgence, which manifests itself in displays of verbal whimsy, the novels she wrote in the 1970s represents the sharpest statement of the feminist position.

5

Genre fiction: Anthony Burgess, William Golding, Robert Nye, Peter Vansittart, John Banville, J. G. Ballard, Michael Moorcock, John Le Carré, P. D. James, Ruth Rendell

The expression, 'the literary novel', has entered common usage in the last twenty years; it is a useful, but unhelpfully restrictive, term. Employed to differentiate novels which have some ambition to be works of art from those which have not but seem to aim only for popular success, it loses value if it excludes from critical consideration novels which belong to particular genres, but which may nevertheless be written with true imagination and artistic integrity. In fact, genres like the historical novel, science fiction, mysteries and the novel of espionage may all yield work of a quality which transcends the limitations of the genre's conventions.

This is most obviously true of the historical novel, if only because so many of the greatest novels of the nineteenth century fell into that category. Yet dull and conventional practitioners have endangered the critical validity of the genre. Most historical novels are tripe, sentimental fantasies which offer no challenge to any reader. Conversely, therefore, the writing of a historical novel offers a peculiar challenge to the novelist for he or she is required to liberate the form from the easy assumptions with which it has become encrusted. At the same time its attractions are obvious: it allows the writer to consider permanent qualities of mind and character simply by setting a distance of time between the novelist and his material; it frees him from the tyranny of the here and now.

Two approaches to the writing of historical fiction seem both possible and fruitful: the first is that which investigates grand politics by means of a scrupulous and detailed re-creation of a particular time. The outstanding modern practitioners of this form have been the American Gore Vidal and the South

African Mary Renault, who in her last novels, the trilogy dealing with Alexander the Great and with the disintegration of his empire after his death, achieved remarkable effects by her manipulation of the point of view and her refusal to sentimentalize or romanticize her material. These novels, which were great popular successes but underrated by many critics, are likely to last longer than many of the books which have won literary prizes.

Both Anthony Burgess (*The Kingdom of the Wicked*) and William Golding (the *Rites of Passage* trilogy) have experimented with historical fiction. Burgess's has his characteristic virtues of erudition and verve. Golding's pastiche enables him to explore the moral implications of action and the development of sensibility.

The second type of historical novel allows its author greater freedom, for it treats history as myth. Novelists like Robert Nye, Peter Vansittart and John Banville are less interested in creating a simulacrum of historical reality than in capturing the essence of an age and in tracing the mythical elements which connect it, psychologically and imaginatively, with modern sensibility. Nye's characteristic theme is the erotic nerve that trembles behind our thoughts, imaginings and actions. His outstanding novel, *Falstaff* (1976) is the masterpiece of this sort of fiction. It is at once homage to Shakespeare and the Elizabethan vitality, and a comic portrayal of the waste land created by power politics. It is a celebration of man and God; its crudities are as much part of the human edifice as the gargoyles are integral to a medieval cathedral. Written in a rich, yet abrupt and incomparably rapid prose that makes no pretence to belong to the age in which the fiction is ostensibly set, it is nevertheless a timeless novel; modern, yet not confined to the twentieth century. It delights in the exuberance of the life-force while keeping the reality of death, and of the fear of death, ever before us.

In like manner Banville and Vansittart span the centuries, Banville, in *Copernicus* (1987) and *Kepler* (1983), explores the birth of modern science during the late Renaissance as a means of determining the relation of the scientific mind to imaginative creation. Vansittart in *The Death of Robin Hood* (1981) and *Parsifal* (1988) pursues, with dazzling imaginative insight, the persistence of myths (the Green Man, the Grail Legend), through the centuries. Like Nye too, they delight in the juxtaposition of different manners, different modes of feeling, in order to attain a more comprehensive revelation of human nature than can normally be presented in more conventional novels. At their worst, all these writers can lapse into mannerism and self-indulgence; at their best they offer a different slant and an enriching experience.

A concern with different modes of thinking and feeling is also manifest in the novels of J. G. Ballard and Michael Moorcock. Both began by writing conventional science fiction; both transcended its barriers to write novels which, retaining the genre's virtues of directness, imaginative freedom and intellectual enquiry, discarded its reliance on arbitrary and whimsical resolution of narrative.

Both Ballard and Moorcock are prolific – at one time Moorcock was writing a novel a month. This is the way they have come up, through the science fiction magazines. It has a curious double consequence. On the one hand, each is capable of writing with a direct lucidity which makes for easy reading; on the other both are capable of mandarin opacity, the result perhaps of fast writing against deadlines: Moorcock's *A Cure for Cancer* (1971), for instance, is, in his own words, 'too pretentious and obscure, too many private jokes, everything I dislike in someone like Nabokov'.

The great strength of these writers is that they look beyond the world of orderly social fiction. They are both conscious of the imminence of a dehumanized world, dominated by technology, a world in which traditional values appear to be obliterated. Neither welcomes this; quite the contrary. Yet they are willing to confront it. Both have at the same time a range which makes it possible for their work to change direction abruptly: Ballard has written a realistic novel, *Empire of the Sun* (1984), about a Japanese internment camp. Moorcock is engaged on a series of novels set in Edwardian England.

They have weaknesses in common too. Both appear to find little difficulty in turning out well-structured and convincing novels; at the same time these seem insufficiently pondered. They have written so much that they can resolve difficulties of narrative by their mastery of structure rather than by the force of imagination.

Moorcock has an exuberance Ballard lacks. Though Ballard is pleased to deploy pop images throughout his fiction, he does so as an act of criticism, revolted by the naive acceptability of his original image. His novels accordingly are rarely affirmative; he is dismayed by the squalid commodity-dominated urban world. He has suggested that 'the writer's job is no longer to put the fiction in . . . people have enough fiction in their lives already'. He sees it as the writer's job to question the subliminal goods which pass for reality. When he employs realistic techniques, he does so as a means of criticism of conventional notions of what is real.

The idea that shadows can assume a superior reality is central to the concept of spy fiction. The unquestioned modern master of this genre is John Le Carre, unquestioned at least since his early rival Len Deighton temporarily deserted the spy novel in favour of thoroughly researched and documented re-creations of war, *Fighter* (1987) and *Bomber* (1970), and alternative history, *SS-GB* (1978).

Le Carré is the legitimate heir of John Buchan and Eric Ambler. Like them, he uses the form of the spy novel as a means of assessing the moral condition of the nation. Like them he is aware of the precarious nature of civilization. Yet he has taken the form further, perhaps beyond a valid point. Whereas Buchan and Ambler characteristically portrayed the murky world of secret politics as an interruption in the decent and orderly lives of their heroes, Le Carré makes it an image sufficient in itself. There is no world beyond it for his characters, who have been so formed and corrupted by their experiences in the secret world that they are incapable of conceiving any decent way of life as a practical possibility. At times Le Carré seems to share this delusion. The Secret Services of which he writes have lost their reason for existence: they have come to protect nothing except themselves.

Yet there is a moral force in Le Carré's fiction, particularly evident in *Tinker, Tailor, Soldier, Spy* (1974) and *Smiley's People* (1980), his best two novels, which makes a great deal of conventional literary fiction seem trivial. If Robert Nye shows how the erotic nerve disturbs and reforms moral attitudes, Le Carré in a very different manner never allows us to forget how the lust for power, even in a stale bureaucratic world, can become a dominating and subversive force.

This is the strength of his fiction, and it is scarcely vitiated

John Le Carré *(Photograph Franta Provaznik)*

P. D. James *(Photograph Richard Watt)*

by the frequently pretentious and convoluted style in which he writes. Le Carré has taken the spy novel so far from being in any normal sense of the term a novel of action that one might more exactly describe his world as one of mandarin inaction. His fondness for the indirect approach makes a virtue of secrecy and of deception of the reader, which serves as a parody of the moral attitudes that he critically dissects.

Science fiction, historical novels and spy novels all lend themselves to formulaic treatment which allows the author to manipulate stereotypes whenever invention flags. Even the best rarely avoid giving off an impression of *déjà lu,* at least in parts. Familiarity of this sort makes for easy reading; nothing is so undemanding as the formula novel. This criticism can be levelled with even more force at the classical English mystery novel, which in the hands of its best practitioners like Agatha Christie, Dorothy L. Sayers and Michael Innes achieved the remarkable feat of rendering even the bloodiest murder abstract. Raymond Chandler claimed to have given murder back to the people who commit it, but he did so by restricting crime to a criminal milieu. P. D. James and Ruth Rendell have avoided this limit while restoring the seriousness of the act of murder.

James writes only orthodox detective stories, scrupulously adhering to convention, creating an intellectual puzzle, which nevertheless do not exclude complexity of emotion. Rendell is extremely prolific, writing police detective stories and psychopathic studies under her own name, and also dense explorations of buried crimes, decorated with Gothic motifs, under the name of Barbara Vine. Both are addicted to an excessive degree to literary allusion – James's police detective is a poet himself, while Rendell's is an omnivorous reader with a remarkable memory. Despite this, both writers have succeeded in reintegrating genre fiction in the mainstream novel. James's last, *A Taste for Death* (1986), could most accurately be described as a novel of character turning on the investigation of a murder; in this it was closer to the Victorian master Wilkie Collins than to Christie and Sayers. Rendell's fecundity and understanding of psychopathic personality recall the Franco-Belgian Simenon, whom André Gide once described as 'the best living French novelist'. Rendell has not perhaps marked out her territory as decisively as Simenon did; but her work is of quality comparable to his.

6

The contemporary scene: Martin Amis, Julian Barnes, Ian McEwan, Peter Ackroyd, Salman Rushdie, Angela Carter, Emma Tennant, William Boyd, Alan Judd, Anita Brookner, Penelope Lively, A. N. Wilson, Graham Swift, Kazuo Ishiguro, Timothy Mo, Peter Carey

Somerset Maugham was fond of remarking that writers whose work commands the attention of posterity are usually drawn from those who were admired in their own time; but he also observed that such admiration could be ephemeral. In *Cakes and Ale* (1951) the narrator says: 'I've been writing for thirty-five years now, and you can't think how many geniuses I've seen acclaimed, enjoy their hour or two of glory, and then vanish into obscurity. I wonder what's happened to them. . . . I wonder if they are still great men in some Italian *pensione*.'

Inevitably some of the younger writers I shall discuss in this chapter may end in whatever is the next century's equivalent of that Italian *pensione*. Inevitably some others who have begun more quietly, whose first books made little stir, will be more appreciated in the future. Picking the outstanding novelists of a generation on the strength of their first few books is like selecting a Derby winner on the evidence of form as a two-year-old: a rash and dodgy business. A few years ago the Book Marketing Council organized a promotion of 'The Twenty Best Young British Novelists'. Already a few of their choices look wilted.

Contemporary success requires a writer to be in tune with his times. Consequently his work may acquire a period flavour which may make it seem dated before it has the chance even to take on a period charm. The first novels of Martin Amis, for example, though evidently the work of a gifted writer, now emit stale gusts of the late 1960s and early 1970s; they are for the moment almost unreadable. It was not till his fourth novel, *Other People* (1981), that Amis began to escape from the limiting condition of being bang up to the minute, of having the ear of his exact contemporaries, and only theirs. These early books, *The Rachel Papers* (1973), *Dead Babies* (1975) and *Success* (1978), combined a shimmer of verbal brilliance with an adolescent desire to shock. This, however, was only a case of joining with other adolescents in shocking their elders; there was nothing to disturb readers of his own generation. They indeed were flattered by the novels, and, since the investigation of human nature was superficial, shrinking from the depiction of serious emotion, these novels were ultimately trivial and unambitious.

What makes Amis interesting, however, is the ability to develop which he has shown. *Other People* itself was an unsatisfactory novel, principally because of its indeterminate centre; but it was disturbing as none of his previous books had been, because he was now admitting to ignorance of certain aspects of personality, which he had formerly presented with a glib assurance.

Money (1984) showed a remarkable, not unexpected, advance. Set partly in a glittering but insubstantial New York, partly in a London that offered a shoddy imitation of New York, it was at once contemporary and timeless. Money is both its theme and title, as it was the theme of *Our Mutual Friend;* and Amis recalls Dickens in the exuberant fecundity of language, in his startling insight and moral seriousness, without, one may say gratefully, being in any way what is conventionally and slackly called Dickensian. Money, Amis perceives, has taken on a life of its own: 'All America was interflexed by computer processors whose roots spread outward from the trunks of skyscrapers until they looped like a web from city to city, sorting, clearing, okaying, denying, denying. Software America sprawled on a humming grid of linkup and lookout, with display screens and logic boards of credit ratings, debt profiles.' Money, he sees, has become metaphysical. People have it without showing it, and, having it, go down into the streets and with imaginary money purchase whatever comes into their heads. This is the atmosphere in which his novel lives and the atmosphere into which he launches his greedy innocent John Self.

The narrative is offered as an exaggerated and comic version of modern life; the characterization is no more than emblematic. The vitality of the novel arises not from incident but from the author's disgusted enjoyment of the world he has summoned into being. This money world is like Coketown in *Hard Times,* a monstrous and inhuman creation which fascinates the author; he responds with zestful loathing.

It is the style which constitutes the book's triumph, because it is the galloping and inventive prose which carries Amis's adoring revulsion from modernity. It has an amazing range. It can carry menace: 'as my cab pulled off FDR drive, somewhere in the early Hundreds, a low-slung Tomahawk full of black guys came sharking out of lane and sloped in fast right across our bows'; a sentence where the rhythm is just right, and the weight rests on that word 'sharking' like a fighter on the balls of his feet. It can accommodate reflection, can convey pathos and self-loathing. It is very funny and intensely visual. Whatever is sick, sad and ugly in modern urban life is caught in this style; its rare moments of beauty too.

Money is a delight to read, even though it is made of material which is disgusting and depressing. Almost everything that is good and natural and loving and lovely in life has been jettisoned; we are looking into the trash cans outside the fast-food eatery of a junk civilization. Yet from this Amis has created an entrancing work of art. There has been no novel from him since, though one sensed that *Money* represented a signing-off, that it was a bridge leading from his clever young man's novels to something deeper and more sympathetic. Whatever form his future fiction takes, one cannot think Martin Amis a candidate for Maugham's Italian *pensione.*

Two writers popularly associated with Amis are Julian Barnes and Ian McEwan. In the case of Barnes the association depends on the known friendship between the two writers, and perhaps on the realization that each is eager to make something new of the novel. Barnes is perhaps the hardest of all his generation to assess. Each of the four novels published under his own name (he also writes detective fiction as Dan Kavanagh) has been markedly individual. There is therefore no such thing as a characteristic Barnes novel. This willingness to experiment is admirable, though it may suggest that Barnes is more interested in technique than in content. Such a suspicion may be unfair; it is perhaps truer to say that, setting himself a different problem, and wishing to explore a new area of experience, in each novel, he has necessarily had to find a new means of writing it. The most original and delightful of his four novels *Metroland* (1981), *Before She Met Me* (1982), *Flaubert's Parrot* (1984) and *Staring At The Sun* (1986) is the third, *Flaubert's Parrot*. The hero, a middle-aged divorced doctor visits Rouen in search of Flaubert memorabilia, and broods on the life of the nineteenth-century master, on the art of fiction and its relation to experience, and on his own history. Some of the chapters, discursive essays, inevitably lack narrative interest; yet the wit, humanity and intelligence of the novel fully compensate for its apparently static nature. Barnes is concerned with the state of art in the late twentieth century, with the question posed by the Czech novelist Milan Kundera: whether we have come to the end of the era of culture. Imaginative fiction has been for almost two centuries the principal verbal means of recording and evaluating emotional experience, and of delineating the individual in relation to society. Every thinking novelist must wonder whether this is still possible. Barnes confronts the question, weighing the autonomy of the work of art against the expectations aroused by the methods and material of sociology.

Ian McEwan made his name with two collections of short stories distinguished for the assured elegance of his manner and the immature nastiness of the content. His first two novels, *The Cement Garden* (1979) and *The Comfort of Strangers* (1981), confirmed that he was a writer of a macabre and disturbing imagination, able to point a sentence with enviable exactness, and adept at the evocation of atmosphere. But they also seemed to be written too glibly, within disappointing limits; in particular, like Martin Amis's early novels, they depended for their success on the reader's willingness to be shocked by their wilful distortion of human nature.

Then for six years he published no fiction, writing principally for television and the cinema. His third novel, *The Child in Time* (1987), though a far less confident piece of

Ian McEwan *(Photograph Tara Heinemann)*

craftsmanship than his first two, being confused in theme and uneven in the writing, nevertheless revealed a humanity and capacity to feel, and to arouse feeling, which had been absent from his earlier work. It is set in the England of the near future, and, dancing in a narrow bridge between fantasy and realism, tries to connect private dramas with public concerns. It belongs to the tradition of the 'Condition of England Novel'. It offers McEwan's view of Thatcher's England, a country teeming with licensed beggars, in which control is exercised in the name of freedom, and where poverty and squalor are to be found everywhere in the midst of affluence. The picture owes as much to the conventions of science fiction, especially in the cinema, as it does to observation or imagination, but it is powerful enough, even at second-hand.

One theme is the disintegration of a politician whose public life, as his wife puts it, has been 'all frenetic compensation for what he took to be an excess of vulnerability'. This is handled dramatically enough, though the effect is weakened when McEwan slides into the whimsy of his early short stories. More remarkable, and certainly more satisfactory, is his treatment of his central character, a young novelist who has lost his daughter, abducted from a supermarket, two years earlier. This tragedy has destroyed his marriage, then led to his own descent into apathy, enlivened only by occasional moments of hope as when he sees a girl in the street who might be his daughter. His state is such that service on a government committee set up to recommend principles of child-training seems to offer him more stimulation than anything in his private life; this makes him an extreme case of alienation. The character's fear, self-disgust and despair are convincingly done, and in two scenes, one with the hero's former wife, the other with his father, McEwan for the first time treats adult emotion with sympathy and understanding.

He remains a writer of considerable gifts who has not yet achieved a satisfactory book. There are signs in *The Child in Time* that he may be about to do so. Yet as long as his characteristic response to the moral problems he poses is a retreat to fantasy, his promise is unlikely to be fulfilled. He is a writer whose development has been retarded by the exaggerated enthusiasm with which his immature work was received.

McEwan's fiction is calculated rather than spontaneous. It suffers from a lack of energy; its ambition is curtailed. These are not charges which could be levelled at Peter Ackroyd or Salman Rushdie who, in the last few years, seem to have overtaken Amis, Barnes and McEwan as the novelists who combine critical and commercial success.

Ackroyd is a dandy, self-conscious, elegant and witty. His work is marked by an extreme artificiality. It is always at some remove from life, and he never leaves the reader in any doubt that he is reading a novel. Despite naturalistic passages, often extremely effective, his inspiration generally appears to be literature rather than life. This impression is reinforced by the knowledge that Ackroyd is also a fine literary critic and biographer, who has written illuminatingly of Ezra Pound and T. S. Eliot. But he is also a poet, with a poet's awareness of mystery.

He has written five novels. The first, *The Great Fire of London,* derived from *Little Dorrit,* was a twentieth-century gloss on Dickens. Yet at the same time it was a highly individual and original work, a haunting novel of modern London – of all contemporary writers only Ackroyd reveals the poetry of modern London. It was followed by *The Last Testament of Oscar Wilde,* which won the Somerset Maugham Award, and *Hawksmoor* (1985) which won the *Guardian Fiction Prize* and the *Whitbread Novel Prize.* Both showed his ability to get outside himself; Ackroyd's novels eschew the thinly disguised autobiography which less ambitious writers make the staple of their fiction. Both showed his talent for pastiche, a characteristic mode of post-modernist fiction, *Hawksmoor* offering a glittering reconstruction of late-seventeenth-century London in its exploration of the life of the architect who was a pupil of Wren and built St Mary Woolnoth and St George's, Bloomsbury. The novel is structurally ingenious, for a modern murder mystery is incorporated in the reconstruction, and the two plots, skilfully intertwined, play off each other. This novel, metaphysically convincing, masterly in its treatment of obsession, is Ackroyd's most assured success.

A similar technique, interweaving past and present, and employing pastiche, is used in *Chatterton* (1987). In one sense this novel raised the question whether Ackroyd's manner would stiffen into mannerism; yet it also, though marred by some grotesque and unconvincing caricature, revealed new aspects of his talent, in particular an ability to evoke tenderness, and a new depth of emotion evident in his treatment of the relationship between the unsuccessful poet Charley Wychwood (obsessed with the image of the dying Chatterton, the 'marvellous boy' who, in the eighteenth century wrote poems in 'old English' which deceived many into thinking them genuine) and his wife and small son. This ability to deal lucidly and unpretentiously with domestic emotions – and it is far more difficult to write well of a marriage than of a murder – suggested an intuitive sensitivity for which nothing in Ackroyd's earlier work had prepared one.

In his most recent novel, *First Light* (1989), echoes of other writers are still to be found, but pastiche has been abandoned. So has London. The setting is Dorset, and Ackroyd has written a novel in which a chief element is the sense of the past as an enduring present, a sense which throws into relief the merely provisional nature of modern urban society, and done this without falling into the portentous solemnity which has afflicted the serious English rural novel since Hardy. The novel's themes are time and the immensity of creation. Its action is concentrated on two sites: an observatory and an archaeological dig. He pictures the heavens spinning away, old forms of life trapped mysteriously under the earth – the buried treasure of race memory – and between them, men and women day to day playing out their little roles in the demanding urgency of brief time. It is the novel of a poet, a speculative book, but it is also comic, for Ackroyd's eye for human oddity is acute. These people in between, the men and women of today, are vividly, tenderly and humorously brought to life.

Ackroyd is a writer who fulfils Nabokov's requirement that the novelist should see the world as 'material for fiction'. He is also one who can legitimately be described as Dickensian: he has the same sense of the strange poetry of life, the same relish in human behaviour, the same awareness that comedy derives from the point of view, and he has learned from him how to give authenticity and vitality to a novel by placing naturalistic, even dull, characters at the centre and creating around them characters conceived and displayed as grotesques, who press in on the central characters and then pull away from them in a joyous celebration of human variety.

If Ackroyd's work is open to the accusation that its success is sometimes endangered by cleverness, Salman Rushdie's is threatened by his verbosity. He is a writer uninhibited by taste and unfettered by judgement. In terms of sales and critical attention he may be considered the outstanding novelist of his generation. Yet his work is extremely uneven. Flashes of observation, moments of strong feeling, yield brilliant passages, which are however too often swallowed up in rhetorical obscurity. Even his most coherent novel, *Midnight's Children*, which won the Booker Prize in 1981, and which is an epic account of the achievement and significance of Indian independence, is vitiated by self-indulgence. Rushdie is a writer who must perhaps be taken on his own terms, at his own estimation indeed, if he is not to be found frequently absurd and incompetent. His admirers praise the brilliance of his imagination; his detractors think that this feeds only off itself, that it is rarely directed outwards at anything, and is therefore, in the end, no more than fancy.

His ambition cannot be doubted. *Shame* (1983) addressed itself to the nature of an Islamic state, but its serious point of inquiry was submerged in a welter of Grand Guignol extravagance, leading to a conclusion as ludicrous as it was disgusting. *The Satanic Verses* (1988) aroused the fury of Muslim fundamentalists. Defence of the book and of Rushdie's right to express his own point of view therefore became a test issue for all who believe in freedom. Naturally enough, this dispute silenced any argument about its literary qualities. This was unfortunate. The sincerity of the book was unquestionable; likewise its ambition. Rushdie explored the nature of good and evil, or set out to do so, highlighting the manner in which they appear interchangeable; but the language employed, veering from the coy and whimsical to the frenetic, was incompetent to realize his ambition. Yet many, before the political dispute burst out, seemed to have mistaken the intention for its achievement. Indeed its initial critical reception suggested that, in a world obsessed with the techniques of public relations and dazzled by their glitter, it was enough to state an intention for it to become reality.

Rushdie is associated with what is called Magic Realism. Coined by a German critic Franz Roh in the 1920s, this term has been most usefully applied to Latin American writers like

Borges, Garcia Marquez, Alejo Carpentier and Mario Vargas Llosa. According to the revised edition of the *Oxford Companion to English Literature,* 'magic realist novels have, typically, a strong narrative drive, in which the recognizably realistic mingles with the unexpected and the inexplicable, and in which elements of dream, fairy-story, or mythology combine .with the everyday, often in a mosaic or kaleidoscopic pattern of refraction and recurrence'. This is indeed a fair description of Rushdie's methods, and he is a conscientious practitioner of the genre, which is perhaps the worst for a writer of his temperament. It affords him endless licence, but what he evidently requires if he is to do justice to his gifts, is a narrow and demanding discipline. Unless he submits to such restraint, it seems likely that his novels will grow ever windier and emptier. At present his fiction flourishes in exuberant fancy, sometimes glittering, sometimes disgusting, sometimes trivial.

The label 'Magic Realist' has at times been attached to Angela Carter and Emma Tennant. It is more appropriate in Carter's case. She is a writer of imagination and wit, who works most happily and inventively improvising on a theme supplied by myth or fairy-tale. She is a writer in the dandy tradition, her novels, the best of which is perhaps *Nights at the Circus* (1984), being inconceivable written in any other manner. Style and theme are perfectly integrated, but this achieved perfection itself represents a limit which denies her a more profound resonance. Her imagination is self-consuming, unable to project itself beyond the immediate work. A great novel alters our understanding of the world beyond itself, changes our perception of that world; for all her imaginative virtuosity Carter fails to make the imaginative connections which render such an extension and deepening of comprehension possible.

Tennant is a more varied writer, and one who has shown herself more capable of interesting development. Early works like *Wild Nights* (1979) and *Alice Fell* (1981) were short, intense, lyrical, working by means of a highly charged impressionistic technique. She had already, however, written *The Bad Sister* (1978), a novel which took as its theme the idea of dual personality and as its literary model James Hogg's remarkable tale of demoniac possession *The True Confessions of a Justified Sinner.* In this novel she experimented with a

Angela Carter

method of indirect, frequently misleading narrative, which she was to employ subsequently in *Woman Beware Woman* (1983), *Black Marina* (1985) and *Two Women of London* (1989) Tennant's fiction is based on the premise that things are both precisely what they seem, and often not at all what they seem. An interpretation of an action is, for her, a fact, but it is not necessarily, and perhaps only rarely, the truth. It is at most a partial truth. Our judgement of people is determined by our own experience and by what other people tell us. These are things worth recording, but they do not in themselves provide us with the means of coming to a true understanding. She realizes that people never see themselves as others see them, and that what is objectively ridiculous may be subjectively important. Her subject is the gap in an individual's understanding of human nature and human behaviour.

Such a subject lends itself to methods of indirect or fallible narration. She brings off the marriage of misperception and revelation most satisfactorily in *Woman Beware Woman*, a novel dealing with a murder in Ireland, with the corrupting or distorting influence of celebrity, and with the possessiveness of love, which is lyrical, dramatic and disturbing. She is now embarked on a sequence of novels called *The Cycle of the Sun* of which only the first two volumes, *The House of Hospitalities* (1987) and *A Wedding of Cousins* (1988), have been published.

Here she has a narrator, Jenny Carter, who can be trusted because she is honest, and yet cannot be trusted because she is ignorant. Even while persuaded that she is telling it as she sees it, and striving to understand the significance of what she reports, we cannot rely on her interpretation because her own experience is limited, and her feelings are both powerful and confused.

In these novels Tennant is concerned to be true to emotional experience and to create the appearance and texture of the social world with fidelity. Yet this fiction also rejects the claims to authority which naturalism, the mode to which it might at first seem to belong, has always made. Her use of the innocent and confused narrator reminds us that the naturalist conventions are themselves a matter of choice, and that the same events would look very different, would indeed be very different, if the point of view was altered. Tennant undermines the authority of naturalism by reminding us that the novelist's choice of angle is always arbitrary; that any interpretation of what happens is partial; and that human beings are more unpredictable and mercurial that fictional conventions ordinarily allow them to be.

Tennant revels in the complexity of experience. It is too early to say whether *The Cycle of the Sun* will display the mastery of structure which alone can reconcile the author's awareness of the arbitrary and haphazard elements of life with a satisfying and integrated aesthetic. At present it can only be called one of the most interesting experiments in contemporary fiction.

Two novelists who have eschewed the temptations of self-conscious style and Magic Realism are William Boyd and Alan Judd. Both write traditional novels in which importance is attached to narrative, characterization, the delineation of society and the elaboration of ethical problems. Both understand the importance of structure. Both, though highly ambitious, may be described as plain novelists.

Boyd's development has been uneven, partly because he has sometimes seemed to misunderstand the nature of his talents. His first novel, *A Good Man in Africa* (1981), could be read as a robust farce, written in a manner poised between Kingsley Amis and Tom Sharpe. Yet the best things in it were comic rather than farcical, closer, that is, to Amis than to Sharpe. Boyd was evidently concerned to explore the question of how people should behave. He was a moralist. The 'good man' of the title was not the hero, the fat lustful diplomat Morgan Leafy, but the Scottish doctor, Murray, who says, 'if I'm interested in anything, it's in seeing a bit of fairness in the world'. Then, in *An Ice-Cream War* (1982), set mostly in East Africa during the First World War, Boyd showed a remarkable ability to depict action – a quality he shares with Judd – and also to organize his material. It was a novel on the grand scale, vivid, vital and ironic. It made it clear that here was a young writer willing to assume the full responsibility of the novelist; concerned not only with how people act, but with how they should act. Only a number of derivative passages, recalling the fiction of the period in which it was set, prevented it from being a complete success.

With his third novel, *Stars and Bars* (1984), Boyd seemed to be taking a wrong turning. This was a strenuous but leaden-footed farce set in the United States; it stopped only just short of being a disaster for a writer of his talent. Yet, oddly, his immersion in American life bore fruit in his next book. Despite a slow – and again derivative – start, *The New Confessions* (1986) was written with a swagger and vitality reminiscent of Saul Bellow and quite without the timorousness of much English fiction. It is a deeply serious book which is also a romance of the twentieth century. The narrator, a film director, John James Todd, is a man of formidable will-power, energy, inventiveness and selfishness; at every point in the novel the course on which he has set himself is bent by the external and malignant forces of history.

His ambition is to film Rousseau's *Confessions*. He sees Rousseau (Jean-Jacques like himself) as 'the first truly honest man' and he pursues his ambition in the face of every imaginable obstacle. The first part of the *Confessions* is actually filmed in Berlin in the 1920s; it is immediately rendered obsolete by the invention of the talkies. Boyd's re-creation of this imaginary film is extraordinary: he makes a film in words which is far more vivid than the film which might have been screened. Writing of his original contempt for the coming of sound in the cinema, Todd said, 'History has proved me wrong. But we have lost as much as we have gained. With sound it is too easy to explain, too easy to be precise. The dangerous edge of ambiguity has gone forever. The potent, multifarious suggestions of the visual image were subjugated to prattle. . . .'

In the age of the mass media, in which Boyd himself is evidently comfortable, he has sought to reassert the supremacy of the novel by showing it to be still capable of just that 'dangerous edge of ambiguity', of carrying the same 'potent multifarious suggestions'. The scale of this novel is Victorian, its ambition likewise, but in its picture of an individual of genius enmeshed in the nets cast around him by the modern world, thwarted by technical developments, and the bland requirements of the mass media, as well as by those permanent human qualities like envy, malice, suspicion, Boyd has written a novel for our time and all time. It is never sentimental. Todd is in his own way a monster: selfish, conceited, callous, ridiculous, mean. But he is also a hero, a remarkable creation. There is a sense of space and time in this novel which is wholly exhilarating.

Alan Judd's first novel, *A Breed of Heroes* (1981), also

stepped outside the compound within which the literary novel can seem confined. The setting was Ulster and the main characters officers in the British Army. A social document of some value, it also depicted a man tormented by conscience and did so with sympathy and humour. The characterization was keen, the narrative compelling and well structured, the determination to examine moral questions as admirable as the discriminating manner in which the examination was conducted. Only a certain matter-of-fact ordinariness about the prose limited the achievement. It is not that one looks for brilliant, or even elegant, prose in a novel; indeed such brilliance or elegance may even be detrimental, for they can draw attention away from the matter. Moreover, inasmuch as the novel is an exploratory, rather than a magisterial, art, it is often desirable that the style in which it is written should follow the hesitating or erratic course of exploration rather than carry the finality of judgement. It was the lack of individuality, with a concomitant lack of precision and economy, and a too ready reliance on stock phrases, which made one wonder if Judd had the capacity for development which the important novelist almost invariably possesses. His second book, *Short of Glory* (1984), a comedy about diplomatic life in Southern Africa, intensified these doubts which were, however, dispelled by *The Noonday Devil* (1987). This is an Oxford novel, very different from the generality of the species. Its subject is accidia, occasioned by the insignificance of modern life. Judd poses the question: 'why should we go on when we find so little worthwhile?' It perplexes all his three chief characters, and if it cannot be said that any of them finds a satisfactory answer, the novel itself supplies that. For it is so well made, so vibrant with life, that it is itself life's justification. The concept of art as a force for reconciliation is not a fashionable one; but in this novel Judd reconciles us to experience. In a very different manner he confronts the same problems as are to be found in a Stanley Middleton novel, and he arrives at a similar answer to Middleton's. Weariness permeates *The Noonday Devil* and yet it offers its own vital response to the fatigue of the soul. It is concerned with loss of faith; yet the work itself is an act of faith in the value of art.

The nature of art is a subject which has been made the theme of fiction by Anita Brookner and Penelope Lively. These are two of the more surprising successes – both have won the Booker Prize – among novelists whose work started to appear in the late 1970s. The surprise rests, not in the nature of their talents, but in the course by which these have come to be revealed. Anita Brookner had already established a high reputation as an art historian before she wrote her first novel, while Penelope Lively was a popular author of children's fiction. Moreover, their first novels, though accomplished, did not seem to promise more than minor achievement.

Brookner's work shows the advantage for the novelist of having a coherent outlook and a consistent method; this gives her books an unmistakable character and flavour. Her tone of voice is analytic, civilized and restrained. Her novels may lack vitality but they compensate by an exquisite precision. Typically, she places a highly educated single woman of middle age at the centre of her novels, and it is through the consciousness of this timid and lonely heroine that the significance of events and other characters is evaluated. Her first subject is solitude resulting from the barriers erected between human beings by differences of taste, disposition and habit. She brought her treatment of this theme close to perfection in *Hôtel du Lac* (1984), her most successful novel. Subsequent work has shown more variety. *Family and Friends* (1985) sought to paint a larger canvas, not convincingly. *A Misalliance* (1986) and *A Friend from England* (1987) reverted to her early manner, in such a way as to suggest that this was hardening into mannerism. The message that life was a grim and depressing business which required the exercise of stoicism if it was to be endured seemed to be conveyed with a despondent self-satisfaction, which did not however exclude a pervasive and corrupting self-pity. *Latecomers* (1988) represented a new departure. Without sacrificing the qualities of seriousness and discrimination, which had made her first novels so distinctive and attractive, and with the same intelligent sensibility, it offered a new sense of the bounty of life. It was her first affirmative novel, one which made it clear that she has found a way out of the cul-de-sac into which she appeared to be heading.

Penelope Lively's fiction has lacked the individuality of Brookner's, perhaps because she gives the impression of writing more easily. Her first adult novels, *The Road to*

Lichfield (1977), *Treasures of Time* (1979), *Judgement Day* (1980), were interesting and agreeable rather than compelling. Their strength lay in the accuracy of observation and the assurance of her moral judgement. *Next to Nature, Art* (1982), a satirical account of an artistic community devoted to the false notion of art as self-expression, revealed an unexpectedly light touch and also a capacity for invigorating scorn. Her work deepened with *According to Mark* (1984), but even this did not prepare one for the quality of *Moon Tiger* (1987). This is the story of a woman's life, based on the theory, or rather on her appreciation, that 'nothing is ever lost, everything can be retrieved, that a lifetime is not linear but instant, that, inside the head, everything happens at once'. So, on her death-bed, the popular historian Claudia Hampton recovers her whole life, 'within her head', composing as she does so a history of the world. She reflects that we all put ourselves at the centre of human experience, while at the same time remaining marginal or non-existent for others; she wrestles with the problem of a God in whose goodness she cannot believe. The willingness to confront fundamental problems of experience, and the author's ability to contain these within a shapely and muscular narrative, make *Moon Tiger* one of the finest novels of the 1980s.

A. N. Wilson has not yet written anything as good, though he resembles Lively more than any other writer. This resemblance, however, lies in a certain facility; both can give the impression of finding it too easy to write novels which are never less than seriously entertaining and interesting. Both are well mannered, conscious that most readers read for pleasure, and that the writer who does not please is unlikely to be read. Wilson is a prolific writer, author of admirable biographies of Belloc and Tolstoy; his novels, however, often appear to have been insufficiently pondered upon. The language, though agreeably flowing, can be slack and undistinguished; the point of view fluctuates, not according to any structural decision, but apparently because this is the easiest way to write a novel; the resolution of the narrative can be glib. His novels suffer from a lack of intellectual rigour, as if they are written primarily for his own amusement.

Yet at his best – *Who Was Oswald Fish* (1981), *Gentlemen in*

England (1985), *The Healing Art* (1980), *Three's Company* (1983), *Incline our Hearts* (1988) – he has a Victorian amplitude and generosity. His faults of slackness and sentimentality may be called Victorian also, but they are redeemed by his Trollopean interest in how people behave, and how they should behave; moreover he has a skill in relating feeling to conduct which recalls that master. Like him again, he is ready to concern himself with large and serious subjects such as morality in public life, the place of religion in society or the nature of biographical truth. His Christianity is that of the Church of England, and it helps to make him a moralist who is not censorious, and a humorist who is never cruel. No one shows better than Wilson how the novelist gains from eschewing oddity, and thus escaping the vanity which almost invariably corrupts the work of the wilfully experimental writer. He is in the central tradition of the English comic novel; he never forgets that the novel is a humane art.

Graham Swift is another writer whose work is profoundly and unmistakably English. *Waterland* (1983), a magical evocation of the secret world of the Fen country, was a masterly and intricate narrative. Swift is acutely aware of the influence of the past on the present, or to be more exact, of how the persistence of the past permeates contemporary experience. In *Out of this World* (1988), his fourth novel, one of the narrators, Harry Beech, a photographic journalist, considers how the twentieth century has moved from sepia to black-and-white to full colour:

'my father's world was brown. The brown of leather and horseflesh and mahogany sideboards. The brown of old brown shires and rutted lanes before the spread of tar. Even the first cameras were little brown boxes, glossy and vernable as violins.' Then: 'picture your father, Sophie, walking down Fleet Street on a grey, wet day in the grey post-war year of 1948. He wears the non-colours that are everywhere around him (like a true news photographer he blends in with his surroundings): grey raincoat, dark suit, dark grey trilby. The cars that pass him are black and grey. The city buildings are charcoal studies: soot and stone. The wet road and the clock-face over the daily telegraph building and the smoke from a train on the Blackfriars line and the grey dome of St Paul's against a grey sky are all the tones of newsprint and photographs.'

And then came

'the new age in which Sophie grew up. Was all that to do with the perfecting of the three-colour emulsion process – as if the world had glimpsed itself in some new and flattering mirror – or was it to do, like rising hemlines and marijuana and rockets into space, with sheer high spirits?'

Alert and responsive to the passing of time, to the influence of the past on perception, to the mood of particular places, Swift writes with controlled vividness. He allies his gift for the illuminating phrase and for the image that makes us see the familiar in a new way to a concern for structure which makes each of his novels a complete and achieved entity. He is undoubtedly one of the writers capable of further development likely to surprise us, one of whom it may be asserted with real confidence, that he will play a large part in the future of the English novel.

If Wilson and Swift may be considered quintessentially English, then Kazuo Ishiguro and Timothy Mo offer evidence of how the English-language novel is now enriched from a diversity of cultures. The former is of Japanese extraction, the latter of Chinese, though both were educated in England. Ishiguro's three novels – *A Pale View of Hills* (1982), *An Artist of the Floating World* (1986) and *The Remains of the Day* (1989) – have all been distinguished by an exquisite precision; he is a writer who works scrupulously within self-imposed limits, achieving his effects by understatement and the adroit deployment of his material. Each of his novels has an unmistakable identity; yet he displays his virtuosity in his use of a different narrative voice in each. *The Remains of the Day,* for instance, is narrated by an elderly English butler. In his portrayal of this character, so different from himself, Ishiguro shows himself a pure novelist. The central question which occupies Mr Stevens, the narrator, is 'what makes a great butler?'. This may seem an extraordinary question for a young novelist to pose at the end of the twentieth century; yet

Kazuo Ishiguro (Photograph Nigel Parry)

Ishiguro uses it in order to be able to ask the far more important question of how a man's life is justified.

Graceful, humorous, subtle and enquiring, Ishiguro is a writer who impresses by his willingness to submerge his own personality and by his fidelity to his material. Each of his novels is thoroughly and perfectly composed; the proportions are always seemly. They acquire a strength and authority from Ishiguro's acceptance of physical realities and from the exactness of his perceptions.

Timothy Mo's early fiction offered some of the same pleasures as Ishiguro's; it was notable for the sharpness of his observation. In *An Insular Possession* (1986) he extended his range. This long historical novel dealing with the founding of Hong Kong and the Opium Wars was dense, competent and compelling in narrative. At the same time some of Mo's previous quality was diluted by conventionally flat characterization and dialogue that was too often expository rather than revealing. Yet the novel was to be praised for its willingness to tackle a great theme, and for Mo's awareness of the influence of public events in shaping individual destiny.

Peter Carey, an Australian novelist, displayed in his Booker Prize-winning *Oscar and Lucinda* (1988) similar awareness of the living influence of the past, and an appreciation of the opportunities to explore enduring truths about human behaviour and sentiments which can be afforded the writer by setting his story beyond the contemporary world. Critics of both these novels might charge Mo and Carey with an evasion of the responsibility of the novelist to portray the society in which he actually lives. The accusation 'escapist' is easily levelled at fiction set in a past which the writer has not experienced himself, at novels which clearly depend on historical research as well as on imagination. That historical novels can be escapist for author and reader alike is of course undeniable. Nevertheless, apart from the fact that many of the greatest novels fall in this category, the author can defend his decision to set his story in a distant time or country by observing that nothing is so ephemeral as the purely contemporary, nothing so quickly out of date as the present; moreover, by putting some distance between himself and his subject, the author can focus on what is enduringly true. Indeed the willingness to regard the past as proper territory for the novelist is in itself an act of faith in the value of fiction as a means of understanding human nature, and as a means of illuminating that understanding. Both *An Insular Possession* and *Oscar and Lucinda* offer evidence of how the serious novelist has manoeuvred the form back into the mainstream of human experience. The affirmation that history is a proper subject for the contemporary novelist is an expression of humanist faith; and if the novel ceases to be a humanist art-form, it will lack vitality, authority and relevance to the human condition. Nothing is more remarkable than the number of novelists considered in this chapter – Barnes, Ackroyd and Boyd are three other obvious examples – who show how the past remains an integral part of modern experience. Nothing offers clearer evidence of faith in the enduring vitality of the novel, of its capacity for endless renewal.

7

Sense and sensibility

Attempts to group novelists together, unavoidable in any survey, are inevitably misleading. They tend to draw attention to what a writer has in common with other writers rather than to any unique quality. Moreover, concentration on themes – that is to say, on the extractable and discussible elements of a novel – may obscure the reality that a novel is composed of words arranged in a certain order to provoke certain feelings. Ultimately a novel is more a matter of sensibility than of sense, the prose rhythms determining the author's success more than any message he may have. The attachment of labels to a writer cannot fail to diminish; Fay Weldon, for example, may legitimately be discussed in terms of feminist politics, such discussion being possible without any note being taken of the wit and vivacity which make her novels delightful. It is as well to remember that if novelists wanted to write tracts, they would not go to the greater trouble of writing novels.

Again any schematic treatment can hardly include novelists who fit into no scheme, especially those whose originality rests not in extravagance but in acuity. One such is David Lodge, a comic master who flirts with categorization, but says 'no' at the last minute. On the evidence of *Changing Places* (1975) and *Small World* (1984), he might seem to belong to the school of campus novelists; on the strength of *How Far Can You Go?* (1980) to the provincial novel. Yet Lodge is set apart by his oblique stance; his relationship to the traditional realism, dominant in both these types of novel, is sceptical. He delights in experimentation with technique to show how manner determines response. He is endlessly playful without ever being less than serious. His concern is the effect of perception on moral judgement. A university professor, who has interpreted continental literary theory, especially French structuralism, for the benefit of English readers, his own novels reveal him to be as sceptical of the validity of theory as he is contemptuous of its absence.

Francis King and David Cook are two writers with little in common except that they produce honest, readable and moving books with enviable regularity. King could be dismissed as an agreeable mainstream writer, of sharp observation and with the talent to evoke physical reality, a good professional, if it was not for an awareness of pain, the pleasure of pain, guilt and the pleasure of guilt, that gives his work a distinctly personal moral flavour. Cook, concerned with the isolation of inadequate individuals in a world they have not made and do not understand, might appear a critic of society. So, in a sense he is, but he is a profounder critic, and a critic of a different order, from novelists like Drabble or Kelman, who suggest that if society was ordered differently, the lot of the unfortunate would be substantially ameliorated. Cook appears to have faith neither in a change of heart nor in new structures; he is a poet of an under-class, or rather of society's rejects, those who would fail and be rejected no matter how the world was arranged. He can be described as a social critic only in so far as he speaks for the unfortunate individual against any social form. He is an antisocial novelist, whose heroes can never be anything but lost.

Yet in any account of the contemporary novel, Lodge, King and Cook are distinguished figures. Only they do not belong; or, in King's case, seem superficially and deceptively to belong too easily to the sort of mainstream fiction that critics are happy to disregard.

Coming to the end of this survey the doubts I indicated at the beginning are intensified. There is no such thing as the novel, only novels. Attempts to squeeze writers into categories distorts their individual achievement as much as any particular paragraph may hope to elucidate it. At the same time it excludes writers of quality because they are not exemplary figures, because they have no single work sufficiently cogent to force an entry, or because they seem to me to have steered up a backwater which precludes interesting development. For one of these reasons or another, admiring readers of such as John Wain, Barry Unsworth, George MacBeth, Alice Thomas Ellis, Lisa St Aubin de Teran, Rose Tremain, Margaret Forster, Michael Levey, Ronald Frame, David Hughes, (Nina Bawden, John Fuller, Hugh Fleetwood and Paul Bailey) will scan this little book in vain. These are all writers of quality; at the least evidence of the rich variety of the novel today. And I could add a longer list of those in whose work many find riches where I discern only dross.

Finally there are the really young, those who have published only one or two novels, who have not yet created any sort of body of work. There is for example James Buchan, whose first novel *A Parish of Rich Women* (1984) setting arid and debilitating self-indulgence in café-society London against war-ravaged Beirut, achieved effects of dislocating brilliance. There is Candia McWilliam, author now of two novels: the first, *A Caseful of Knives* (1988), overloaded with jewelled phrases, nevertheless showed rare ability to handle a complex structure and to manipulate the point of view to artistic effect; the second, *A Little Stranger* (1989), added to these qualities a grasp of character. In both novels she displayed a dazzling understanding of the influence of perception and moral perspective on action. Matthew Yorke (*The March Fence*, 1988) writes of physical work with rate authority and of adolescent guilt with sympathy. Nigel Watts (*The Life Game,* 1989) has shown himself capable of integrating philosophical discussion in narrative. Helen Harris (*Playing-Fields in Winter*, 1986 and *Angel Cake*, 1987), Jeannette Winterson (*Oranges are not the Only Fruit,* 1985 and *The Passion*, 1987), Monique Charlesworth (*Life Class,* 1988), Hilary Mantel (*Eight Months on Ghazzah Street,* 1988) are all novelists whose promise has already been confirmed by significant achievement.

There are perhaps a couple of hundred people outside America who write novels in the English language which merit serious critical attention. Any survey is selective. This has dwelled for the most part on novels whose authors carry a British passport, with only passing reference to others such as Brian Moore or Ruth Prawer Jhabvala or Nadine Gordimer whose work seemed especially relevant to the theme of a particular chapter. This has meant that inadequate consideration has been given to Australians like Thomas Keneally and Peter Carey, Indians like Anita Desai and Canadians like Robertson Davies or Margaret Atwood. Moreover the whole corpus of Black African writing has been ignored. It would have required a chapter to itself, and, within the limit of length imposed, that was not possible.

We may have advanced beyond a crossroads in the history of the English novel. If the road leading to self-conscious experiment has not been taken, it is still possible to argue that the reliance on complacent naturalism, which some thought to characterize the post-war English novel, is equally a thing of the past. It was possible to exaggerate the extent of that reliance, salutary to remember that C. P. Snow was an exact contemporary of Anthony Powell and Henry Green, that John Braine's *Room at the Top* (1957) was published in the same year as Muriel Spark's first novel. The novel has always been a loose and capacious term; for every discernible trend it has been possible to find contemporary counter-currents. So, today, while it may seem that the future of the novel is to appeal to an international readership, it does not follow that this excludes the local or particular writer. The Japanese author Shusako Endo is an example of one who has achieved international success without diluting his native culture.

It remains certain, however, that the novel can only flourish if it remains aware of its own definition as a piece of news. Novelty may rest in subject-matter or manner, and the degree of novelty may be hard to identify. It must nevertheless be there if the book is not to stink of stale fish. All the writers whom I have considered here are to some extent at least conscious of their responsibility in this respect. They respond to changing social values and the changing shape of society with new perceptions. They are aware, even the most apparently naturalistic of them, that reality can no longer be complacently defined. They are aware too of paradox: the concept of character has been challenged by physiological and psychological advances and theories; yet perception of 'real' character remains central to the way we try to understand the world. It is the novelist's task to explore this paradox.

The duty of exploration may indeed be taken as the imperative which drives the novelist. The novel is an exploratory form, seeking out routes by which author and reader can together come to a truer understanding of the world. Dealing in imperfections, the novelist understands that this understanding can itself be never other than imperfect. This is why it is not a form suited to the ideologically committed. Orwell described it as 'a Protestant form'; inasmuch as his phrase retains value, it has lost its sectarian significance. But it reminds us that the writing of a novel is an act of individual judgement, or rather that it is composed of myriads of such acts. Reading a novel is of the same order. Both writing and reading depend on the use of the imagination. This is true whether the novel superfically seems to set out to achieve a close resemblance to everyday life or whether it flies far away from it. Neither mode is admirable in itself; it depends on how it is done. On the whole, I have restricted myself to writers whose work I admire, in some degree at least; therefore, by and large, the imagination seems to me to be well used by most of the novelists I have considered, the delights offered by them to be enriching.

Select bibliography

This bibliography only includes first editions of works produced by the authors since 1970.

ACKROYD, **Peter** (1949–)

The Great Fire of London (Hamish Hamilton, 1982).
The Last Testament of Oscar Wilde (Hamish Hamilton, 1983).
Hawksmoor (Hamish Hamilton, 1985).
Chatterton (Hamish Hamilton, 1987).
First Light (Hamish Hamilton, 1989).

AMIS, **Kingsley** (1922–)

Girl, 20 (Cape, 1971).
Dear Illusion (Covent Garden Press, 1972).
The Riverside Villas Murder (Cape, 1973).
Ending Up (Cape, 1974)
The Alteration (Cape, 1976).
Jake's Thing (Hutchinson, 1978).
The Darkwater Hall Mystery (Tragara Press: Edinburgh, 1978).
Russian Hide-and-Seek: a melodrama (Hutchinson, 1980).
Collected Short Stories (Hutchinson, 1980).
Stanley and the Women (Hutchinson, 1984).
The Old Devils (Hutchinson, 1986).
Collected Short Stories (Hutchinson, 1987).
Difficulties with Girls (Hutchinson, 1988).
Crime of the Century (Hutchinson, 1989).

AMIS, **Martin** (1949–)

The Rachel Papers (Cape, 1973).
Dead Babies (Cape, 1975).
Success (Cape, 1978).
Other People: a mystery story (Cape, 1981).
Money (Cape, 1984).
Einstein's Monsters (Cape, 1987).
London Fields (Cape, 1989).

BAILEY, **Paul** (1937–)

Trespasses (Cape, 1970)
A Distant Likeness (Cape, 1973).
Peter Smart's Confessions (Cape, 1977).
Old Soldiers (Cape, 1980).
Gabriel's Lament (Cape, 1986).

BALLARD, **J.G.** (1930–)

The Atrocity Exhibition (Cape, 1970).
Crash (Cape, 1973).
Vermilion Sands (Cape, 1973).
Concrete Island (Cape, 1974).
High Rise (Cape, 1975).
Low flying Aircraft and other stories (Cape, 1976).
The Unlimited Dream Company (Cape, 1979).
Myths of the Near Future (Cape, 1982).
Empire of the Sun (Gollancz, 1984).
The Day of Creation (Gollancz, 1987).
Running Wild (Hutchinson, 1988).

BARNES, Julian (1946–)

Metroland (Cape, 1980).
Duffy (Cape, 1980). *(under
pseudonym* **Dan Kavanagh***)*
Fiddle City (Cape, 1981). *(under
pseudonym* **Dan Kavanagh***)*
Before She Met Me (Cape, 1982).
Flaubert's Parrot (Cape, 1984).
Putting the Boot In (Cape, 1985)
(under pseudonym **Dan Kavanagh***)*
Staring at the Sun (Cape, 1986).
Going to the Dogs (Viking,
1987). *(under pseudonym* **Dan
Kavanagh***)*
*History of the World in 10½
Chapters* (Cape, 1989).

BARSTOW, Stan (1928–)

A Season with Eros (short stories)
(Michael Joseph, 1971).
The Right True End (Michael
Joseph, 1976).
A Brother's Tale (Michael Joseph,
1980).
The Glad Eye and other stories
(Michael Joseph, 1984).
Just You Wait and See (Michael
Joseph, 1986).
B-Movie (Michael Joseph, 1987).

BAWDEN, Nina (1925–)

The Birds on the Trees (Longman,
1970).
Anna Apparent (Longman, 1972).
George Beneath a Paper Moon
(Allen & Unwin, 1974).
Afternoon of a Good Woman
(Macmillan, 1976).
Familiar Passions (Macmillian,
1979).
Walking Naked (Macmillan, 1981).
The Ice House (Macmillan, 1983).
Circles of Deceit (Macmillan, 1987)

BOYD, William (1952–)

A Good Man in Africa (Hamish
Hamilton, 1981).
*On the Yankee Station and other
stories* (Hamish Hamilton, 1981).
An Ice-Cream War (Hamish
Hamilton, 1982).
Stars and Bars (Hamish Hamilton,
1984).
School Ties (Hamish Hamilton,
1985).
The New Confessions (Hamish
Hamilton, 1987).

BRADBURY, Malcolm (1932–)

The History Man (Secker &
Warburg, 1975).
*Who Do You Think You Are?:
stories and parodies* (Secker &
Warburg, 1976).
Rates of Exchange (Secker &
Warburg, 1982).
Why Come to Slaka? (Secker &
Warburg, 1986).
Cuts (Hutchinson, 1987).

BRAINE, John (1922–86)

Stay With Me Till Morning (Eyre
& Spottiswoode, 1970).
The Queen of a Distant Country
(Methuen, 1972).
The Pious Agent (Methuen, 1975).
Waiting for Sheila (Methuen,
1976).
Finger of Fire (Methuen, 1977).
One and Last Love (Methuen,
1981).
The Two of Us (Methuen, 1984).
These Golden Days (Methuen,
1985).

BROOKE-ROSE, Christine (1926–)

Thru (Hamish Hamilton, 1975).
Amalgamemnon (Carcanet, 1984).
Xorandor (Carcanet, 1986).

BROOKNER, Anita (1928–)

A Start in Life (Cape, 1981).
Providence (Cape, 1982).
Look at Me (Cape, 1983).
Hôtel du Lac (Cape, 1984).
Family and Friends (Cape, 1985).
A Misalliance (Cape, 1986).
A Friend from England (Cape, 1987).
Latecomers (Cape, 1988).
Lewis Percy (Cape, 1989).

BUCHAN, James (1954–)

A Parish of Rich Women (Hamish Hamilton, 1984).
Davy Chadwick (Hamish Hamilton, 1987).

BURGESS, Anthony (1917–)

MF (Cape, 1971).
The Napoleon Symphony (Cape, 1974).
Inside Mr Enderby (Heinemann, 1975).
The Clockwork Testament, or Enderby's End (Hart-Davis MacGibbon, 1974).
Moses (Dempsey & Squires, 1976).
Beard's Roman Woman (Hutchinson, 1977).
Abba Abba (Faber, 1977).
1985 (Hutchinson, 1978).
Man of Nazareth (McGraw-Hill: New York, 1979. Magnum: London).
Earthly Powers (Hutchinson, 1980).
The End of the World News (Hutchinson, 1982).

Enderby's Dark Lady (Hutchinson, 1984).
The Kingdom of the Wicked (Hutchinson, 1985).
The Pianoplayers (Hutchinson, 1986).
Any Old Iron (Hutchinson, 1989).

BYATT, A.S. (1936–)

The Virgin in the Garden (Chatto & Windus, 1978).
Still Life (Chatto & Windus, 1985).
Sugar and other stories (Chatto & Windus, 1987).

CAREY, Peter (1943–)

War Crimes (University of Queensland Press, 1979).
Exotic Pleasures (Pan Books, 1981).
Fat Man in History (Faber, 1980).
Bliss (Faber, 1981).
Illywhacker (Faber, 1985).
Oscar and Lucinda (Faber, 1988).

CARTER, Angela (1940–)

Love (Hart Davis, 1971).
The Infernal Desire Machines of Doctor Hoffman (Hart Davis, 1972).
Fireworks: nine profane pieces (Quartet, 1974).
The Passion of New Eve (Gollancz, 1977).
The Bloody Chamber and other stories (Gollancz, 1979).
Black Venus's Tale (Next Editions, with Faber, 1980).
Nights at the Circus (Chatto & Windus, 1984).
Black Venus (Chatto & Windus, 1985).

CHARLESWORTH, **Monique**
(1951–)

The Glasshouse (Hamish
Hamilton, 1986).
Life Class (Hamish Hamilton,
1988).

COETZEE **J.M.** (1940–)

Dusklands (Raven Press, 1974;
Secker & Warburg, 1982).
In the Heart of the Country (Secker
& Warburg, 1977).
Waiting for the Barbarians (Secker
& Warburg, 1980).
Life and Times of Michael K
(Secker & Warburg, 1983).
Foe (Secker & Warburg, 1986).

COOK **David** (1940–)

Albert's Memorial (Secker &
Warburg, 1972).
Happy Endings (Alison Press,
1974).
Walter (Secker & Warburg, 1978).
Winter Doves: a love story (Alison
Press, 1979).
Sunrising (Secker & Warburg,
1984).
Missing Persons (Secker &
Warburg, 1986).
Crying Out Loud (Secker &
Warburg, 1988).

DRABBLE, **Margaret** (1939–)

London Consequences with
Johnson, B.S. and others.
(Greater London Arts
Association, for the Festival of
London, 1972).
The Needle's Eye (Weidenfeld &
Nicolson, 1972).
The Realms of God (Weidenfeld &
Nicolson, 1975).

The Ice Age (Weidenfeld &
Nicolson, 1977).
The Middle Ground (Weidenfeld &
Nicolson, 1980).
The Radiant Way (Weidenfeld &
Nicolson, 1987).
A Natural Curiosity (Viking,
1989).

ELLIS, **Alice Thomas** (1932–)

The Sin Eater (Duckworth, 1977).
The Birds of the Air (Duckworth,
1980).
The 27th Kingdom (Duckworth,
1982).
The Other Side of the Fire
(Duckworth, 1983).
Unexplained Laughter
(Duckworth, 1986).
Home Life (Duckworth, 1986).
Clothes in the Wardrobe
(Duckworth, 1987).
Skeleton in the Cupboard
(Duckworth, 1988).

FLEETWOOD, **Hugh** (1944–)

A Painter of Flowers (Hamish
Hamilton, 1972).
Foreign Affairs (Hamish Hamilton,
1973).
The Girl Who Passed for Normal
(Hamish Hamilton, 1973).
An Artist and a Magician (Hamish
Hamilton, 1977).
The Beast (Hamish Hamilton,
1978).
The Godmother (Hamish
Hamilton, 1979).
Fictional Lines (Hamish Hamilton,
1980).
A Young Fair God (Hamish
Hamilton, 1981).
A Dance to the Glory of God
(Hamish Hamilton, 1983).

Order of Death (Hamish
Hamilton, 1983).
A Dangerous Place (Hamish
Hamilton, 1985).
Paradise (Hamish Hamilton, 1986).
The Past (Hamish Hamilton,
1987).
*Man Who Went Down With His
Ship* (Hamish Hamilton, 1988).
The Witch (Hamish Hamilton,
1989).

FORSTER, **Margaret** (1938–   )

Fenella Phizackerly (Secker &
Warburg, 1970).
Mr Bone's Retreat (Secker &
Warburg, 1971).
The Seduction of Mrs Pendlebury
(Secker & Warburg, 1974).
Mother, Can You Hear Me?
(Secker & Warburg, 1979).
*The Bride of Lowther Fell: a
romance* (Secker & Warburg,
1980).
Marital Rights (Secker &
Warburg, 1981).
Private Papers (Chatto, 1986).
Have the Men Had Enough?
(Chatto, 1989).

FRAME, **Ronald** (1953–   )

Winter Journey (Bodley Head,
1984).
*Watching Mrs Gordon and other
stories* (Bodley Head, 1985).
*A Long Weekend with Marcel
Proust* (seven short stories and a
novel) (Bodley Head, 1986).
Sandmouth People (Bodley Head,
1987).
A Woman of Judah (Bodley Head,
1987).
Penelope's Hat (Hodder &
Stoughton, 1989).

FULLER, **John** (1930–   )

The Last Bid (Deutsch, 1975).
Flying to Nowhere (Salamander
Press: Edinburgh, 1983).
Tell it Me Again (Chatto, 1988).

GOLDING, **William** (1911–   )

*The Scorpion God: three short
novels* (Faber, 1971).
Darkness Visible (Faber, 1979).
Rites of Passage (Faber, 1980).
The Paper Men (Faber, 1984).
Close Quarters (Faber, 1987).
Fire Down Below (Faber, 1989).

GORDIMER, **Nadine** (1923–   )

A Guest of Honour (Cape, 1971).
Livingstone's Companions (Cape,
1972).
The Conservationist (Cape, 1974).
Selected Stories (Cape, 1975).
Some Monday for Sure
(Heinemann, 1976).
Late Bourgeois World (Cape, 1976).
World of Strangers (Cape, 1976).
Occasion for Loving (Cape, 1978).
Lying Days (Cape, 1978).
Burger's Daughter (Cape, 1979).
A Soldier's Embrace (Cape, 1980).
July's People (Cape, 1981).
Something Out There (Cape, 1984).
Sport of Nature (Cape, 1987).

GORDON, **Giles** (1940–   )

*Pictures from an Exhibition: short
stories* (Allison & Busby, 1970).
The Umbrella Man (Allison &
Busby, 1971).
About a Marriage (Allison &
Busby, 1972).
Girl with Red Hair (Wildwood
House, 1974).

Farewell, Fond Dreams: short stories (Hutchinson, 1975).
100 Scenes from Married Life: A Selection (Hutchinson, 1976).
Enemies (Harvester, 1977).
Couple: short stories (Sceptre Press, 1978).
The Illusionist and other fictions (Harvester, 1978).
Ambrose's Vision (Harvester, 1980).

GRAY, **Alasdair** (1934–)

The Comedy of the White Dog (Print Studio Press, 1979).
Lanark: a life in four books (Canongate, 1981).
Unlikely Stories, Mostly (Canongate, 1983).
1982, Janine (Cape, 1984).
The Fall of Kelvin Walker (Canongate, 1985).
Lean Tales (short stories by Scottish writers) James Kelman, Alasdair Gray and Agnes Owens (Cape, 1985).

GREENE, **Graham** (1904–)

Collected Stories (Heinemann – Bodley Head, 1972).
The Honorary Consul (Bodley Head, 1973).
The Human Factor (Bodley Head, 1978).
Dr Fischer of Geneva (Bodley Head, 1980).
Monsignor Quixote (Bodley Head, 1982).
The Tenth Man (Bodley Head, 1985).
The Captain and the Enemy (Reinhardt, 1988).

HARRIS, **Helen** (1955–)

Playing Fields in Winter (Hutchinson, 1986).
Angel Cake (Hutchinson, 1987).

HOPE, **Christopher** (1944–)

A Separate Development (Routledge & Kegan Paul, 1981).
Private Parts and other stories (Routledge & Kegan Paul, 1982).
Kruger's Alp (Heinemann, 1984).
The Hottentot Room (Heinemann, 1986).
Black Swan (Hutchinson, 1987).
My Chocolate Redeemer (Heinemann, 1989).

HUGHES, **David** (1930–)

Memories of Dying (Constable, 1976).
A Genoese Fancy (Constable, 1979).
The Imperial German Dinner Service (Constable, 1983).
The Pork Butcher (Constable, 1984).
But for Bunter (Heinemann, 1985).

ISHIGURO, **Kazuo** (1954–)

A Pale View of Hills (Faber, 1982).
An Artist of the Floating World (Faber, 1986).
The Remains of the Day (Faber, 1989).

JAMES **P.D.** (1920–)

Shroud for a Nightingale (Faber, 1971).
An Unsuitable Job for a Woman (Faber, 1972).
The Black Tower (Faber, 1975).

Death of an Expert Witness (Faber, 1977).
Innocent Blood (Faber, 1980).
The Skull Beneath the Skin (Faber, 1982).
A Taste for Death (Faber, 1986).
Devices and Desires (Faber, 1989).

JHABVALA, **Ruth Prawer** (1927–)

An Experience of India: short stories (John Murray, 1971).
A New Dominion (John Murray, 1972).
Heat and Dust (John Murray, 1975).
In Search of Love and Beauty (John Murray, 1985).
How I Became a Holy Mother, and other stories (John Murray, 1976).
Out of India: selected stories (John Murray, 1987).
Three Continents (John Murray, 1987).

JOHNSTON, **Jennifer** (1930–)

The Captains and the Kings (Hamish Hamilton, 1972).
The Gates (Hamish Hamilton, 1973).
How Many Miles to Babylon? (Hamish Hamilton, 1974).
Shadows on Our Skin (Hamish Hamilton, 1977).
The Old Jest (Hamish Hamilton, 1979).
The Christmas Tree (Hamish Hamilton, 1981).
The Railway Station Man (Hamish Hamilton, 1984).
Fool's Sanctuary (Hamish Hamilton, 1987).

JORDAN, **Neil** (1950–)

Night in Tunisia and other stories (Writers' and Readers' Publishing Cooperative, 1979).
The Past (Cape, 1980).
The Dream of a Beast (Chatto & Windus, 1983).

JUDD, **Alan** (1947–)

Breed of Heros (Hodder & Stoughton, 1981).
Short of Glory (Hodder & Stoughton, 1984).
Noonday Devil (Hutchinson, 1987).
Tango (Hutchinson, 1989).

KELMAN, **James** (1946–)

Not, Not While the Giro: and other stories (Polygon, 1983).
The Busconductor Hines (Polygon, 1984).
A Chancer (Polygon, 1985).
Lean Tales (short stories by Scottish writers) James Kelman, Alasdair Gray and Agnes Owens. (Cape, 1985).
Greyhound for Breakfast: short stories (Secker & Warburg, 1987).
A Disaffection (Secker & Warburg, 1989).

KING, **Francis** (1923–)

A Domestic Animal (Longman, 1970).
Flights: two short novels (Hutchinson, 1973).
A Game of Patience (Hutchinson, 1974).
The Needle (Hutchinson, 1975).
Hard Feelings and other stories (Hutchinson, 1976).

Danny Hill (Hutchinson, 1977).
The Action (Hutchinson, 1978).
Indirect Method, and other stories
(Hutchinson, 1980).
Act of Darkness (Hutchinson,
1983).
Voices in an Empty Room
(Hutchinson, 1984).
One is a Wanderer (Hutchinson,
1985).
Frozen Music (Hutchinson, 1987).
The Woman Who Was God
(Hutchinson, 1988).

LE CARRE, **John** (1931–)

The Native and Sentimental Lover
(Hodder & Stoughton, 1971).
Tinker, Tailor, Soldier, Spy
(Hodder & Stoughton, 1974).
The Honourable Schoolboy
(Hodder & Stoughton, 1977).
Smiley's People (Hodder &
Stoughton, 1980).
The Quest for Karla (Hodder &
Stoughton, 1982).
The Little Drummer Girl (Hodder
& Stoughton, 1983).
The Perfect Spy (Hodder &
Stoughton, 1986).
The Russia House (Hodder &
Stoughton, 1989).

LESSING, **Doris** (1919–)

Briefing for a Descent into Hell
(Cape, 1971).
The Story of a Non-Marrying Man:
stories (Cape, 1972).
The Summer Before the Dark
(Cape, 1973).
The Memoirs of a Survivor
(Octagon Press, 1975).
Collected Stories:

I.   *To Room Nineteen* (Cape,
     1978).
II. *The Temptation of Jack*
     Orkney (Cape, 1978).
Canopus in Argos: Archives
  1. *Shikasta* (Cape, 1978).
  2. *The Marriages Between*
      Zones Three, Four and Five
      (Cape, 1980).
  3. *The Sirian Experiments*
      (Cape, 1981).
  4. *The Making of the*
      Representative Planet 8
      (Cape, 1982).
  5. *The Sentimental Agents of*
      the Volyen Empire (Cape,
      1983).
The Diaries of Jane Somers (*under*
pseudonym **Jane Somers**)
  1   *The Diary of a Good*
      Neighbour (Michael Joseph,
      1983).
  2   *If the Old Could . . .*
      (Michael Joseph, 1984).
(In one volume as *Diaries of*
Jane Somers (Michael Joseph,
1984)).
The Good Terrorist (Cape, 1985).
The Fifth Child (Cape, 1988).

LEVEY, **Michael** (1927–)

Tempting Fate (Hamish Hamilton,
1982).
An Affair on the Appian Way
(Hamish Hamilton, 1984).
Men at Work (Hamish Hamilton,
1989).

LIVELY, **Penelope** (1933–)

The Road to Lichfield
(Heinemann, 1977).
Nothing Missing but the Samovar:
stories (Heinemann, 1978).

Treasures of Time (Heinemann, 1979).
Judgement Day (Heinemann, 1980).
Next to Nature, Art (Heinemann, 1982).
Perfect Happiness (Heinemann, 1983).
Corruption, and other stories (Heinemann, 1984).
According to Mark (Heinemann, 1984).
Pack of Cards: stories, 1978–86 (Heinemann, 1986).
Moon Tiger (Deutsch, 1987).
Passing On (Deutsch, 1989).

LODGE, **David** (1935–)

Out of the Shelter (Macmillan, 1970).
Changing Places (Secker & Warburg, 1975).
How Far Can You Go? (Secker & Warburg, 1980).
Small World (Secker & Warburg, 1984).
Nice Work (Secker & Warburg, 1988).

MACBETH, **George** (1932–)

The Transformation (Gollancz, 1975).
The Samurai (Quartet, 1976).
The Survivor (Quartet, 1977).
The Seven Witches (W.H. Allen, 1978).
The Born Losers (New English Library, 1981).
A Kind of Treason (Hodder & Stoughton, 1981).
Anna's Book (Cape, 1983).
The Lion of Pescara (Cape, 1984).
Dizzy's Woman (Cape, 1986).

MCEWAN, **Ian** (1948–)

First Love, Last Rites (stories) (Cape, 1975).
In Between the Sheets (stories) (Cape, 1978).
The Cement Garden (Cape, 1978).
The Comfort of Strangers (Cape, 1981).
The Child in Time (Cape, 1987).

MCILVANNEY, **William** (1936–)

Docherty (Allen & Unwin, 1975).
Laidlaw (Hodder & Stoughton, 1977).
The Papers of Tony Veitch (Hodder & Stoughton, 1983).
The Big Man (Hodder & Stoughton, 1985).
Remedy is None (Drew, 1989).
Walking Wounded (Hodder & Stoughton, 1989).

MACLAVERTY, **Bernard** (1942–)

Lamb (Cape, 1980).
A Time to Dance and other stories (Cape, 1982).
Cal (Cape, 1983).
Secrets and other stories (Allison & Busby, 1984).
The Great Profundo and other stories (Cape, 1987).

MCWILLIAM, **Candia** (1956–)

A Case of Knives (Bloomsbury, 1988).
A Little Stranger (Bloomsbury, 1989).

MANTEL, **Hilary** (1952–)

Every Day is Mother's Day (Chatto, 1985).

Vacant Possession (Chatto, 1986).
Eight Months on Ghazzah Street
(Viking, 1988).
Fludd (Viking, 1989).

MASSIE, **Allan** (1938–)

*Change and Decay in All Around I
See* (Bodley Head, 1978).
The Last Peacock (Bodley Head,
1980).
The Death of Men (Bodley Head,
1981).
One Night in Winter (Bodley
Head, 1984).
Augustus (Bodley Head, 1986).
A Question of Loyalties
(Hutchinson, 1989).

MIDDLETON, **Stanley** (1919–)

Apple of Eve (Hutchinson, 1970).
Brazen Prison (Hutchinson, 1971).
Cold Gradations (Hutchinson,
1972).
A Man Made of Smoke
(Hutchinson, 1973).
Holiday (Hutchinson, 1974).
Distractions (Hutchinson, 1975).
Still Waters (Hutchinson, 1976).
Ends and Means (Hutchinson,
1977).
Two Brothers (Hutchinson, 1978).
In A Strange Land (Hutchinson,
1979).
The Other Side (Hutchinson,
1980).
Blind Understanding (Hutchinson,
1982).
Entry into Jerusalem (Hutchinson,
1982).
The Daysman (Hutchinson, 1984).
Valley of Decision (Hutchinson,
1985).
After Dinner Sleep (Hutchinson,
1986).

After a Fashion (Hutchinson,
1987).
Recovery (Hutchinson, 1988).

MO, **Timothy** (1950–)

The Monkey King (Deutsch, 1978).
Sour Sweet (Deutsch, 1982).
An Insular Possession (Chatto &
Windus, 1986).

MOORCOCK, **Michael** (1939–)

The Chinese Agent (Hutchinson,
1970).
The Eternal Champion
(Mayflower, 1970).
*Phoenix in Obsidian (the second
book of The Eternal Champion)*
(Mayflower, 1970).
The Winds of Limbo (Sphere,
1970).
The Books of Corum:
  1. *The Knight of the Swords*
     (Mayflower, 1971).
  2. *The Queen of Swords*
     (Mayflower, 1971).
*Rituals of Infinity, or, The New
Adventures of Doctor Faustus*
(Arrow, 1971).
Dancers At the End of Time
  1. *An Alien Heat* (MacGibbon
     & Kee, 1972).
  2. *The Hollow Lands*
     (MacGibbon & Kee, 1975).
  3. *The End of All Songs* (Hart
     Davis, 1976).
*Breakfast in the Ruins: a novel of
inhumanity* (New English Library,
1972).
The Warlord of the Air (New
English Library, 1971).
A Cure for Cancer (Allison &
Busby, 1971).
Elric of Melnibone (Hutchinson,
1972).

The Sleeping Sorceress (New English Library, 1972).

The English Assassin (Allison & Busby, 1972).

The Chronicle of Prince Corum and the Silver Hand
1. *The Bull and the Spear* (Allison & Busby, 1973).
2. *The Oak and the Ram* (Allison & Busby, 1973).
3. *The Sword and the Stallion* (Allison & Busby, 1974).

The Black Corridor (Mayflower, 1973).

The Jade Man's Eyes (Unicorn Bookshop: Brighton, 1973).

The Chronicles of Castle Brass:
1. *Count Brass* Vol I. (Mayflower, 1973).
2. *The Champion of Garathorm* (Mayflower, 1973).
3. *The Quest for Tanelorn* (Mayflower, 1975).

The Land Leviathan (Quartet, 1974).

The Distant Suns (Unicorn Bookshop: Brighton, 1975).

The Adventures of Una Persson and Catherine Cornelius in the Twentieth Century (Quartet, 1976).

The Sailor on the Seas of Fate (Quartet, 1976).

The Time of Hawklords (with **Michael Butterworth**) (Aidan Ellis: Henley-on-Thames, 1976).

The Condition of Musak: a Jerry Cornelius novel (Allison & Busby, 1977).

The Transformation of Miss Mavis Ming: a romance of the end of time (W.H. Allen, 1977).

Gloriana, or, the Unfulfill'd Queen (Allison & Busby, 1978).

The History of the Runestaff (Hart Davis, 1979).

(contains: *The Jewel in the*

Skull; The Mad Dog Amulet; The Sword of Dawn).

The Entropy Tango: a comic romance (New English Library, 1981).

Byzantium Endures (Secker & Warburg, 1981).

The Great Rock 'n' Roll Swindle (Virgin, 1981).

The Steel Tsar (Granada, 1981).

The Brothel in Rosenstrasse (New English Library, 1982).

The War Hound and the Worlds Pain (New English Library, 1982).

The Golden Barge (New English Library, 1983).

The Russian Intelligence (New English Library, 1983).

The Bone of the Black Sword (Panther, 1984).

The Laughter of Carthage (Secker & Warburg, 1984).

The Weird of the White Wolf (Panther, 1984).

The Vanishing Tower (Granada, 1983).

The City of Autumn Stars (Grafton, 1986).

The Opium General (Grafton, 1986).

The Dragon in the Sword (Grafton, 1987).

Mother London (Secker & Warburg, 1988).

MOORE, **Brian** (1921–)

Fergus (Cape, 1971).

The Revolution Script (Cape, 1971).

Catholics (Cape, 1972).

The Great Victorian Collection (Cape, 1975).

The Doctor's Wife (Cape, 1976).

The Mangan Inheritance (Cape, 1979).

The Temptation of Eileen Hughes (Cape, 1981).

Cold Heaven (Cape, 1983).
The Black Robe (Cape, 1985).
The Colour of Blood (Cape, 1987).

MURDOCH, Iris (1919–   )

A Fairly Honourable Defeat
(Chatto & Windus, 1970).
An Accidental Man (Chatto &
Windus, 1971).
The Black Prince (Chatto &
Windus, 1971).
*The Sacred and Profane Love
Machine* (Chatto & Windus, 1974).
A Word Child (Chatto & Windus,
1975).
Henry and Cato (Chatto &
Windus, 1976).
The Sea, The Sea (Chatto &
Windus, 1978).
Nuns and Soldiers (Chatto &
Windus, 1980).
The Philosopher's Pupil (Chatto &
Windus, 1983).
The Good Apprentice (Chatto &
Windus, 1985).
The Book and the Brotherhood
(Chatto & Windus, 1987).
The Message to the Planet (Chatto
& Windus, 1989).

NAIPAUL, V.S. (1932–   )

In a Free State (Deutsch, 1971).
Guerillas (Deutsch, 1975).
A Bend in the River (Deutsch,
1979).
Finding the Centre: two narratives
(Deutsch, 1984).
The Enigma of Arrival (Viking,
1987).

NYE, Robert (1939–   )

Falstaff (Hamish Hamilton, 1976).
Marlin (Hamish Hamilton, 1978).

Faust (Hamish Hamilton, 1980).
The Voyage of the Destiny
(Hamish Hamilton, 1982).
Facts of Life and other fictions
(Hamish Hamilton, 1983).

POWELL, Anthony (1905–   )

Books Do Furnish a Room
(Heinemann, 1971).
Temporary Kings (Heinemann,
1973).
Hearing Secret Harmonies
(Heinemann, 1975).
O, How the Wheel Becomes It
(Heinemann, 1983).
The Fisher King (Heinemann, 1986).

READ, Piers Paul (1941–   )

The Professor's Daughter (Secker &
Warburg: Alison Press, 1971).
The Upstart (Secker & Warburg,
1973).
Polonaise (Secker & Warburg:
Alison Press, 1976).
A Married Man (Secker &
Warburg, 1979).
The Villa Golitsyn (Secker &
Warburg, 1981).
A Free Frenchman (Secker &
Warburg, 1986).
A Season in the West (Alison
Press, 1988).

RENDELL, Ruth (1930–   )

A Guilty Thing Surprised
(Hutchinson, 1970).
No More Dying Then
(Hutchinson, 1971).
One Across, Two Down
(Hutchinson, 1971).
Murder Being Once Done
(Hutchinson, 1972).

Some Lie and Some Die
(Hutchinson, 1973).
The Face of Trespass (Hutchinson,
1974).
Shake Hands for Ever
(Hutchinson, 1975).
The Fallen Curtain and other stories
(Hutchinson, 1976).
A Demon in My View
(Hutchinson, 1976).
A Judgement in Stone
(Hutchinson, 1977).
A Sleeping Life (Hutchinson, 1978).
Make Death Love Me
(Hutchinson, 1979).
Means of Evil and other stories
(Hutchinson, 1979).
The Lake of Darkness
(Hutchinson, 1980).
Put On By Cunning (Hutchinson,
1981).
The Master of the Moor
(Hutchinson, 1982).
The Fever Tree and other stories
(Hutchinson, 1982).
The Speaker of Mandarin
(Hutchinson, 1983).
The Killing Doll (Hutchinson, 1984).
The Tree of Hands (Hutchinson,
1984).
An Unkindness of Ravens
(Hutchinson, 1985).
*The New Girl Friend and other
stories* (Hutchinson, 1985).
Live Flesh (Hutchinson; 1986).
Heartstones (Hutchinson, 1986).
A Dark Adapted Eye (*under
pseudonym* **Barbara Vine**)
(Viking, 1986).
Talking to Strange Men
(Hutchinson, 1987).
Collected Short Stories
(Hutchinson, 1987).
A Fatal Inversion (*under pseudonym*
Barbara Vine) (Viking, 1987).

The House of Stairs (*under
pseudonym* **Barbara Vine**, 1988).
The Bridesmaid (Hutchinson,
1989).

RUSHDIE, **Salman** (1947–)

Grimus (Gollancz, 1975).
Midnight's Children (Cape, 1981).
Shame (Cape, 1983).
The Satanic Verses (Viking, 1988).

SILLITOE, **Alan** (1928–)

A Start in Life (W.H. Allen,
1970).
Travels in Nihilon (W.H. Allen,
1971).
Raw Material (W.H. Allen, 1972).
Men, Women and Children (W.H.
Allen, 1973).
The Flame of Life (W.H. Allen,
1974).
The Widower's Son (W.H. Allen,
1976).
The Storyteller (W.H. Allen,
1979).
The Second Chance (stories)
(Cape, 1981).
Her Victory (Granada, 1982).
The Lost Flying Boat (Granada,
1983).
Down from the Hill (Granada,
1984).
Out of the Whirlpool (Hutchinson,
1987).
The Far Side of the Street (short
stories) (W.H. Allen, 1988).
The Open Door (Grafton, 1989).

SMITH, **Iain Crichton** (1928–)

Survival Without Error (stories)
(Gollancz, 1970).
My Last Duchess (Gollancz, 1971).
The Black and the Red (stories)
(Gollancz, 1973).

Goodbye, Mr Dixon (Gollancz, 1974).
The Village (stories) (Club Leabhar: Inverness, 1976).
The Hermit and other stories (Gollancz, 1977).
An End of Autumn (Gollancz, 1978).
Murdo, and other stories (Gollancz, 1981).
A Field Full of Folk (Gollancz, 1982).
The Search (Gollancz, 1983).
Mr Trill in Hades, and other stories (Gollancz, 1984).
The Tenement (Gollancz, 1985).
In the Middle of the Wood (Gollancz, 1987).

SPARK, **Muriel** (1918–)

The Driver's Seat (Macmillan, 1970).
Not to Disturb (Macmillan, 1971).
The Hothouse by the East River (Macmillan, 1973).
The Abbess of Crewe (Macmillan, 1974).
The Takeover (Macmillan, 1976).
Territorial Rights (Macmillan, 1979).
Loitering with Intent (Bodley Head, 1981).
The Only Problem (Bodley Head, 1984).
The Stories of Muriel Spark (Bodley Head, 1986).
A Far Cry From Kensington (Constable, 1988).

ST AUBIN DE TERAN, **Lisa** (1953–)

Keepers of the House (Cape, 1982).
Slow Train to Milan (Cape, 1983).

The Tiger (Cape, 1984).
The Bay of Silence (Cape, 1986).
Black Idol (Cape, 1987).
The Marble Mountain and other stories (Cape, 1989).

STOREY, **David** (1933–)

Pasmore (Longman, 1972).
A Temporary Life (Allen Lane, 1973).
Life Class (Cape, 1974).
Saville (Cape, 1976).
A Prodigal Child (Cape, 1982).
Present Times (Cape, 1984).

SWIFT, **Graham** (1949–)

The Sweetshop Owner (Allen Lane, 1980).
Shuttlecock (Allen Lane, 1981).
Learning to Swim and other stories (London Magazine Editions, 1982).
Waterland (Heinemann, 1983).
Out of This World (Viking, 1988).

TENNANT, **Emma** (1937–)

The Crack of Time (Cape, 1973). (Reprinted as *The Crack Faber*, 1980).
The Last of the Country House Murders (Cape, 1974).
Hotel de Dream (Gollancz, 1976).
The Bad Sister (Gollancz, 1978).
Wild Nights (Cape, 1979).
Alice Fell (Cape, 1980).
Queen of Stones (Cape, 1982).
Women Beware Women (Cape, 1983).
Black Marina (Faber, 1985).
The Adventures of Robin, by Herself (Faber, 1986).
The House of Hospitalities (Viking, 1987).

A Wedding of Cousins (Viking, 1988).
Magic Drum (Viking, 1989).
Two Women of London (Faber, 1989).

THOMAS, **D. M.** (1935–)

The Flute Player (Gollancz, 1979).
Birthstone (Gollancz, 1980).
The White Hotel (Gollancz, 1981).
Ararat (Gollancz, 1983).
Swallow (Gollancz, 1984).
Sphinx (Gollancz, 1986).
Summit (Gollancz, 1987).

TREMAIN, **Rose** (1943–)

Sadler's Birthday (Macdonald, 1976).
Letter to Sister Benedicta (Macdonald, 1978).
The Cupboard (Macdonald, 1981).
The Colonel's Daughter and other stories (Hamish Hamilton, 1984).
The Swimming Pool Season (Hamish Hamilton, 1985).
The Garden of the Villa Mollini and other stories (Hamish Hamilton, 1987).
Restoration (Hamish Hamilton, 1989).

TREVOR, **William** (1928–)

Miss Gomez and the Brethren (Bodley Head, 1971).
The Ballroom of Romance and other stories (Bodley Head, 1972).
The Last Lunch of the Season (Covent Garden Press, 1973).
Elizabeth Alone (Bodley Head, 1974).
Angels at the Ritz and other stories (Bodley Head, 1975).

The Children of Dynmouth (Bodley Head, 1976).
Lovers of Their Time and other stories (Bodley Head, 1978).
The Distant Past and other stories (Poolbeg Press: Swords, Ireland, 1979).
Other People's Worlds (Bodley Head, 1980).
Beyond the Pale (Bodley Head, 1981).
Fools of Fortune (Bodley Head, 1983).
News from Ireland and other stories (Bodley Head, 1986).
Nights at the Alexandra (Hutchinson. 1987).
The Silence in the Garden (Bodley Head, 1988).

UNSWORTH, **Barry** (1930–)

The Hide (Gollancz, 1970).
Mooncranker's Gift (Allen Lane, 1973).
Big Day (Michael Joseph, 1976).
Pascali's Island (Michael Joseph, 1980).
The Rage of the Vulture (Granada, 1982).
Stone Virgin (Hamish Hamilton, 1985).
Sugar and Rum (Hamish Hamilton, 1988).

VANSITTART, **Peter** (1920–)

Landlord (Peter Owen, 1970).
Quintet (Peter Owen, 1976).
Lancelot (Peter Owen, 1979).
The Death of Robin Hood (Peter Owen, 1980).
Three Six Seven: memoirs of a very important man (Peter Owen, 1983).

Aspects of Feeling (Peter Owen, 1986).

WAIN, John (1925–)

A Winter in the Hills (Macmillan, 1970).
The Life Guard, and other stories (Macmillan, 1971).
King Caliban and Other Stories (Macmillan, 1978).
The Pardoner's Tale (Macmillan, 1978).
Young Shoulders (Macmillan, 1982).
Where the Rivers Meet (Hutchinson, 1988).

WATTS, Nigel (1957–)

Life Game (Hodder & Stoughton, 1989).

WELDON, Fay (1931–)

Down Among the Women (Heinemann, 1971).
Female Friends (Heinemann, 1975).
Remember Me (Hodder & Stoughton, 1976).
Little Sisters (Hodder & Stoughton, 1977).
Praxis (Hodder & Stoughton, 1979).
Puffball (Hodder & Stoughton, 1980).
Watching Me Watching You (short stories) (Hodder & Stoughton, 1981).
The President's Child (Hodder & Stoughton, 1982).
The Life and Loves of a She-Devil (Hodder & Stoughton, 1983).
Polaris, and other stories (Hodder & Stoughton, 1985).
The Shrapnel Academy (Hodder & Stoughton, 1986).

The Heart of the Country (Hutchinson, 1987).
The Hearts and Lives of Men (Heinemann, 1987).
The Rules of Life (Hutchinson, 1987).
The Leader of the Band (Hodder & Stoughton, 1988).
The Cloning of Joanna May (Collins, 1989).

WILSON, A.N. (1950–)

The Sweets of Pimlico (Secker & Warburg, 1977).
Unguarded Hours (Secker & Warburg, 1978).
Kindly Light (Secker & Warburg, 1979).
The Healing Art (Secker & Warburg, 1980).
Who Was Oswald Fish? (Secker & Warburg, 1981).
Wise Virgin (Secker & Warburg, 1982).
Scandal (Hamish Hamilton, 1983).
Gentlemen in England (Hamish Hamilton, 1985).
Love Unknown (Hamish Hamilton, 1986).
Incline Our Hearts (Hamish Hamilton, 1988).

WINTERSON, Jeannette

Oranges Are Not the Only Fruit (Pandora, 1985).
Boating for Beginners (Methuen, 1985).
The Passion (Bloomsbury, 1987).
Sexing the Cherry (Bloomsbury, 1989).

YORKE, Matthew (1958–)

The March Fence (Viking, 1988).

Index